Dedication: To every person who bravely attempts new things, hungrily seeks to learn new tools, and who actively comes to the table desiring to make new friends. I welcome you to the social mix and am so excited that you are about to join the social conversation. This book is dedicated to you.

About the author:

Kathryn Rose is a Certified Social Media strategist and trainer, specializing in integration of new technologies in marketing strategies, Search Engine Optimization (SEO), Mobile Marketing and Social Media development and training to help clients maximize their visibility online. A featured speaker on New Technology Marketing at the Real Estate University, Ladies Who Launch, Loan Officer Magazine, and the International Social Media Association, Kathryn spent 15 years as a top marketing and sales professional in Residential Real Estate and Finance, most recently as top salesperson for Credit Suisse where she was responsible for over $100m per year in sales. Kathryn also developed the world's first mobile autoresponder, MobiReply, a cutting edge mobile marketing product which helps clients seamlessly integrate their current email marketing campaigns with a dynamic mobile marketing platform.

Her 20-plus years in marketing, sales and public relations uniquely positions her to offer cross platform sales driving strategies to clients. She is a founding member of the International Social Media Association, the professional association for Social Media Marketers. Kathryn has helped countless entrepreneurs, small and large organizations utilize online and social media marketing for business retention and growth. Kathryn is the author of 6 books on social media for business: Step by Step Guides to Facebook, Twitter, Linkedin and SEO/Video for business as well as *The Parent's Guide to Facebook and the Grandparent's Guide to Facebook.*

Connect with Kathryn on:

Facebook : http://facebook.com/katrose

Twitter: http://twitter.com/katkrose

Linkedin: http://linkedin.com/in/katkrose

Table of Contents

Chapter 1: Why have a Linkedin™ Profile? 5

Chapter 2: How to Get Started On Linkedin 9

Chapter 3: Creating your Linkedin Profile 12

Chapter 4: The Anatomy of a Linkedin Profile 17

Chapter 5: Privacy Settings on Linkedin 33

Chapter 6: Creating Connections 44

Chapter 7: Managing Introductions 54

    Connecting Through Groups 62

    Connections through outside networks 63

Chapter 8: Beginning the Conversation 65

Chapter 9: Grow Your Sphere Of Influence Through Linkedin Groups 67

Chapter 10: Adding Applications 77

Chapter 11: Linkedin Events 87

Chapter 12: Add video to your profile 92

Chapter 13: The Power of Recommendations 96

Chapter 14: Using Questions and Answers 102

Chapter 15: Using Linkedin Ads 107

Chapter 16: Listing your company on Linkedin 116

Chapter 17: Following Companies, Users or Discussions . 120

Chapter 18: Creating Your Linkedin Strategy 127

Chapter 19: Checklist for Success 129

Chapter 1: Why have a Linkedin™ Profile?

LinkedIn is an amazing business development tool and has huge potential to help your business create massive traffic, leads and newfound revenue streams. Plus, LinkedIn is the most effective of all the social networking sites for someone looking to manage his or her career.

LinkedIn is absolutely the best social network for making business connections. Your professional network of trusted contacts gives you an advantage in your business or career, and is one of your most valuable assets. LinkedIn exists to help you make better use of your professional network and help the people you trust in return.

If you are a business owner, a professional, or an employee of a company, the answer is the same as to why LinkedIn is important to you.

Linkedin is fast becoming THE place for your potential clients, competition, future employees and future employers to find the best and brightest. You simply cannot ignore the power of social media sites to improve your business. To round out your social media presence you need to establish a branded and optimized Linkedin profile.

As with other social media platforms such as Twitter and Facebook, LinkedIn has added some interesting features recently: you can send images, article excerpts, blog posts and other content to your professional connections in much the same way that you would with your personal connections on other social networks.

Not sure if LinkedIn is right for you? Consider these statistics:

- LinkedIn has over 80 million members in over 200 countries.

- A new member joins LinkedIn approximately every second, and about half of their members are outside the U.S.

- Executives from all Fortune 500 companies are LinkedIn members.

See the chart below for specific demographics compared to some of the leading business publications:

	LinkedIn Comp | Reach	WSJ Comp | Reach	Forbes Comp | Reach	BusinessWeek Comp | Reach
Male / Female	54% / 46%	64% / 36%	67% / 33%	58% / 42%
Average Age	43	50	50	48
Average HHI	$107,278	$99,911	$96,003	$95,255
■ $100k+	51.8 | 6,467,000	43.2 | 3,599,000	39.5 | 3,442,000	38.9 | 1,440,000
■ $150k+	23.1 | 2,888,000	22.7 | 1,892,000	20 | 1,741,000	19.2 | 712,000
Education				
■ College/Post Grad	77.6 | 9,697,000	69.7 | 5,802,000	65.5 | 5,709,000	66.6 | 2,468,000
■ Post College Graduate	39.8 | 4,967,000	37.7 | 3,135,000	33.6 | 2,926,000	36.2 | 1,341,000
Senior-Level Management				
■ EVP/SVP/VP	6.2 | 770,000	5.3 | 439,000	3.7 | 324,000	5.1 | 189,000
■ Senior Management	14.1 | 1,761,000	15.8 | 1,318,000	12.8 | 1,117,000	13.2 | 490,000
■ Middle Management or above	32.1 | 4,012,000	26.6 | 2,216,000	23.6 | 2,058,000	26.7 | 991,000

Source. Nielsen Online @Plan, Summer 2009

If this is your target market OR you would like to:

- ➢ **Connect with other professionals**
- ➢ **Find a position, employees or professional services**

> **Be found for joint ventures, strategic alliances and other business propositions**

Linkedin **is** for you!

Chapter 2: How to Get Started On Linkedin

Now that you know how important Linkedin can be to your online presence, let's go over some important things before you get started on the network.

Just like you would do if you were considering any new marketing initiative, you should ask yourself some questions: (take a moment to write the answers in the space provided)

1. What do I hope to accomplish on the network? Am I looking to increase my business? Find JV partners? Find a job? Answers to these questions will help you in formulating your Linkedin profile and plan.

_____

_____

_____

_____

_____

_____

2. Who are my target audience/partner candidates/ connections that can help me with job placement/jv's/client sales? Answers to these questions will help you when searching for connections and in joining groups.

_____

_____

_____

_____

_____

3. What is it about ME that would make them want to connect? What are my skills, what problems can I solve? What can I offer to the conversation that will make these people want to work with/hire me?

_____

_____

_____

_____

Like any social network, Linkedin is a NETWORK. I tell clients all the time that you have to work these platforms just like a regular in-person networking event. You have to establish a relationship-- a *trust*, then and only then, will they want to do business with you. In fact, if you abuse Linkedin connections you can be kicked off the network! It is important to have a goal for connecting and plan for implementing the steps to your goal in order to be successful.

Now that you have your goals in place, let's get started with setting up your Linkedin profile.

Chapter 3: Creating your Linkedin Profile

To get started you must set up a profile on Linkedin :

Go to http://Linkedin.com

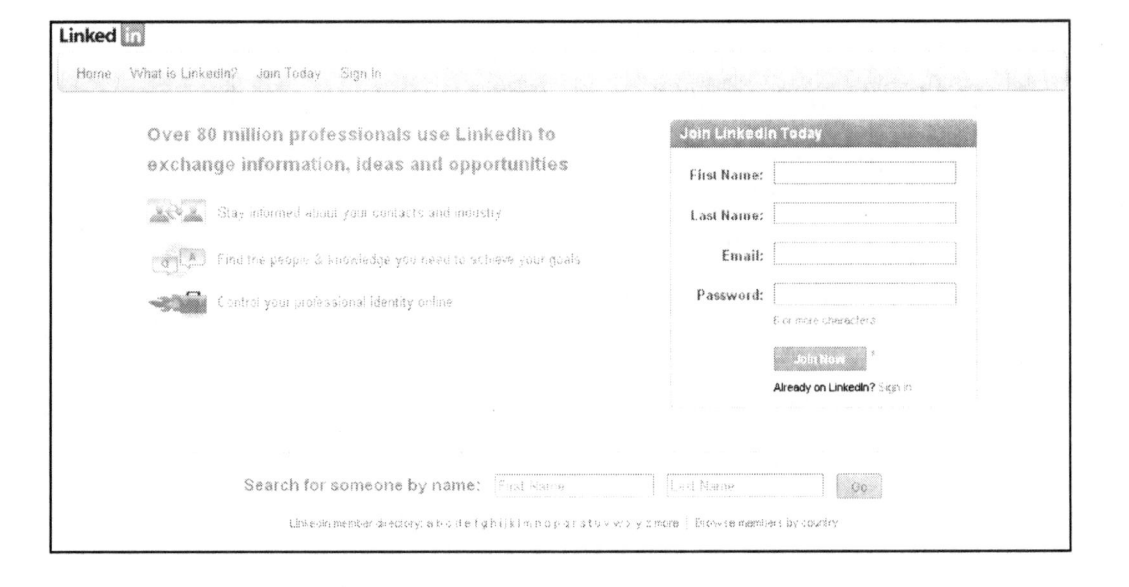

Note: The registration page might vary in appearance, depending on whether you're signing up with or without an invitation, but the registration process is essentially the same.

You will be asked to start to fill in your profile information.

Fill in all the information on this screen, if you are employed, your company name, etc. Then you must activate your account via the link sent to you in your email.

Once you sign in, you will be asked to import your contacts from other email sources to make it easier to find connections.

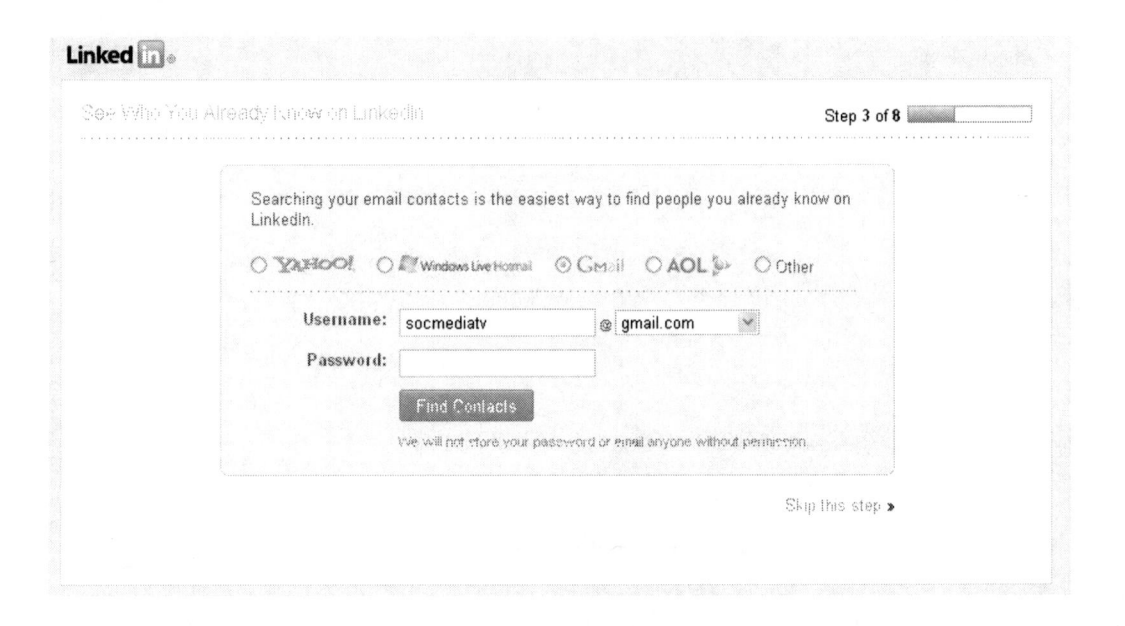

I don't usually recommend doing this at this point because it is advisable to have your profile set up prior to inviting people to connect. However, once you have your profile set up properly you may wish to upload your business contact addresses to get your connections set up more quickly.

If you don't want to upload your entire email database, you can enter specific addresses:

You're Almost Done

Connect to more people you know and trust.
Enter email addresses of colleagues and friends to invite and connect.
Separate each address with a comma.

Send Invitations

Skip this step »

You will then be asked to choose your plan. Linkedin is a
free site but also offers a paid option. I recommend you
begin with a free account to learn how to use the
platform. There are reasons to consider upgrading as you
will see later in this book but I believe it's best to get
started with a free account before you commit to a
monthly fee.

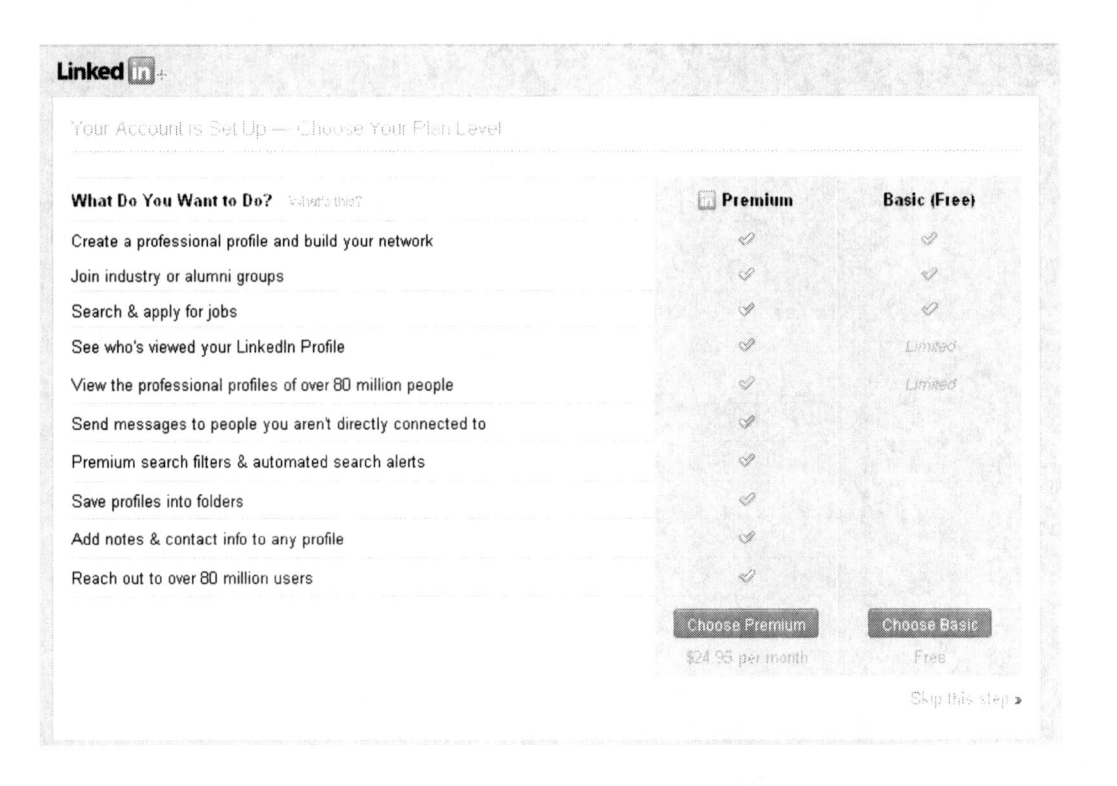

Once again you will be asked if you want to begin to connect using your email address list. Again, I recommend you hold off until you get your profile optimized.

Chapter 4: The Anatomy of a Linkedin Profile

When you sign on to the site for the first time after you confirm your email address you will see a screen that looks like this:

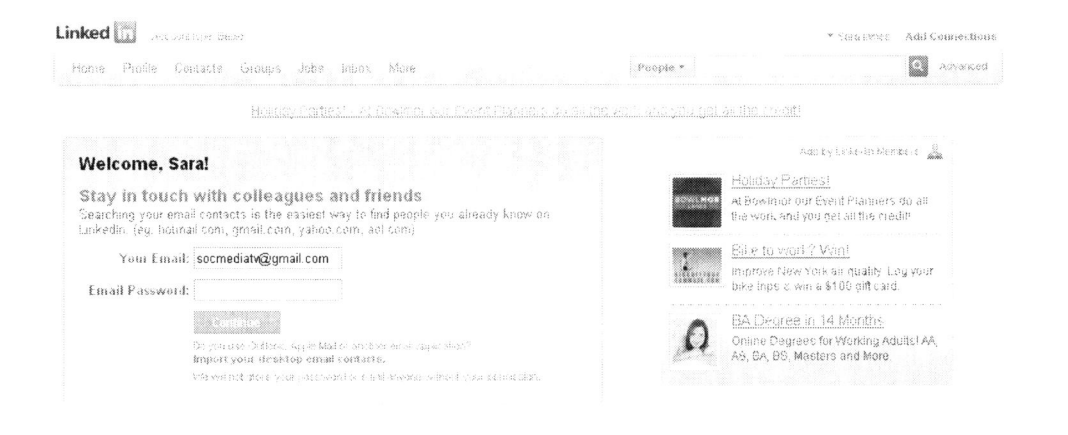

Once you set up an actual profile and begin to connect, the "home page" will look like this:

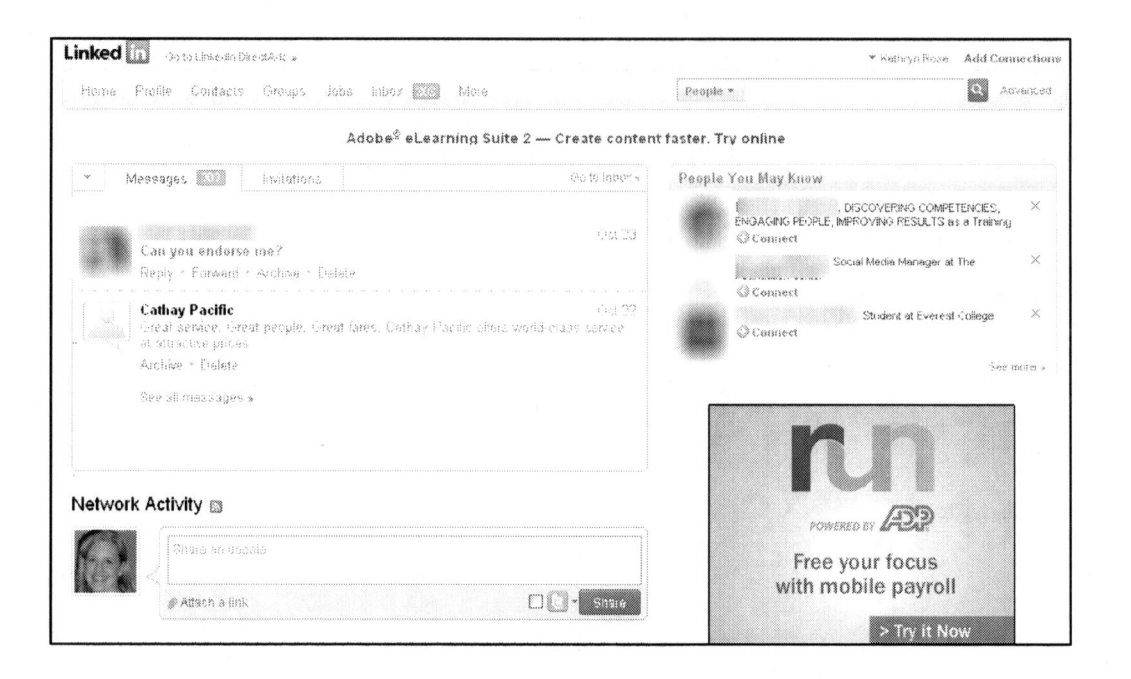

"Home" is where you land when you login to the site. It is a "news feed" type of area. It will display people you may know, any messages, invitations, profile updates, recommendations, etc.

To begin setting up your profile, go to the top navigation bar and click the "profile" link.

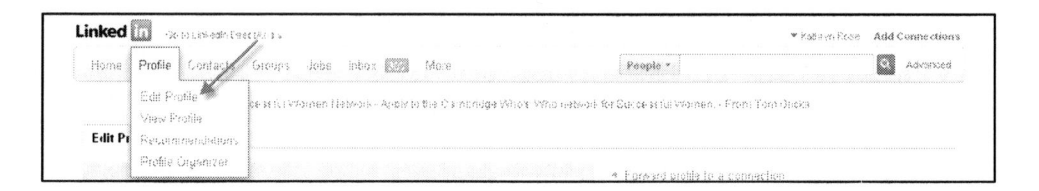

Click on "edit profile" and this screen comes up:

The first thing you need to do is upload a PERSONAL

photo. Many people use their company logo. That is not recommended because people do business with people! Adding a photo provides an emotional connection. There is an option on Linkedin to add your company listing to their directory as I will cover in a later chapter. That area is the appropriate place to upload your logo.

<u>Word of advice</u>: Make the photo professional. This site is dedicated to professionals who even in business casual aren't wearing t-shirts, ball caps, or Hawaiian prints.

If you can't take time to put a decent photo up, it isn't realistic to expect fellow professionals to take the time to get to know a faceless contact. This is your first impression for possible connections looking at your profile, make sure it's a good one.

The next step is to click on "edit" next to your name:

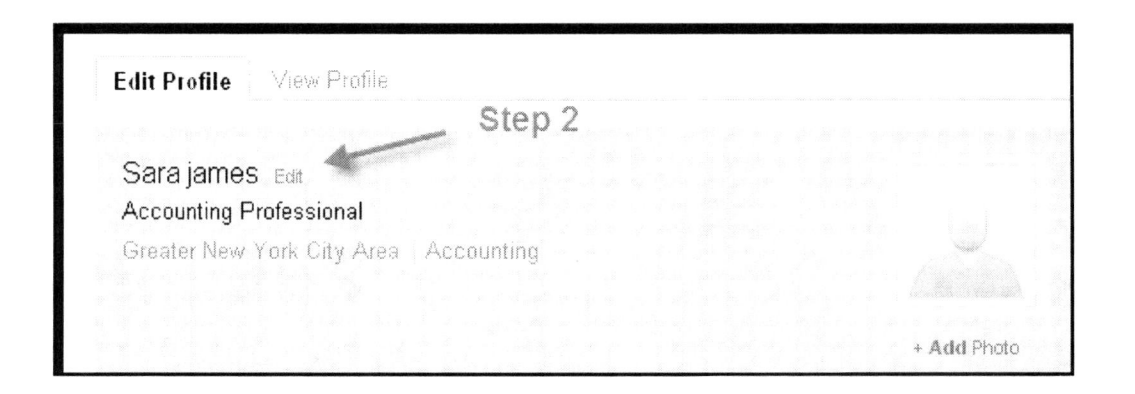

Then you will come to this screen:

Here is where you need to put some thought into your

profile. Using keyword rich content for your headline and

position descriptions will make it easier to find you when people search for your profile inside LinkedIn and also via internet search engines.

For example, in the "Professional Headline" area resist the urge to just type in your normal title like "Owner" or "Vice President." Linkedin is a powerful authority site for Google and other search engines. If you "Google" your name or that of a colleague most likely you will come up with a Linkedin profile. Also, people go on Linkedin to find professional services, partners etc. You want people to be able to find you for what you actually DO not what your title says. So, for example, if Sara here is an accountant instead of typing in "President" she would type in, Corporate Accountant specializing in helping mid to large size companies. She could also type in just keywords, Corporate Accountant | Small Firm Accounting Company | Bookkeeping Services and the like. Keep in mind however that there is a 120 character limit.

In compiling this headline it is helpful to ask yourself a few questions:

1. What would your ideal client type in to look for you?

2. What type of business do you want to attract?

3. When you search Linkedin for professionals in your field, who comes up first and what do they have listed as their headline?

Compile a list of descriptive keywords to use in your profile for maximum visibility. Use this area to write down your top keywords:-

_____

_____

_____

_____

_____

_____

The same principle applies to the current and past position titles. Use keywords, this way if someone goes to

Linkedin (which they often do) and types in "Corporate Accountant" she has a higher likelihood of coming up on the first page.

Linkedin will show your profile completeness status on the left of your profile:

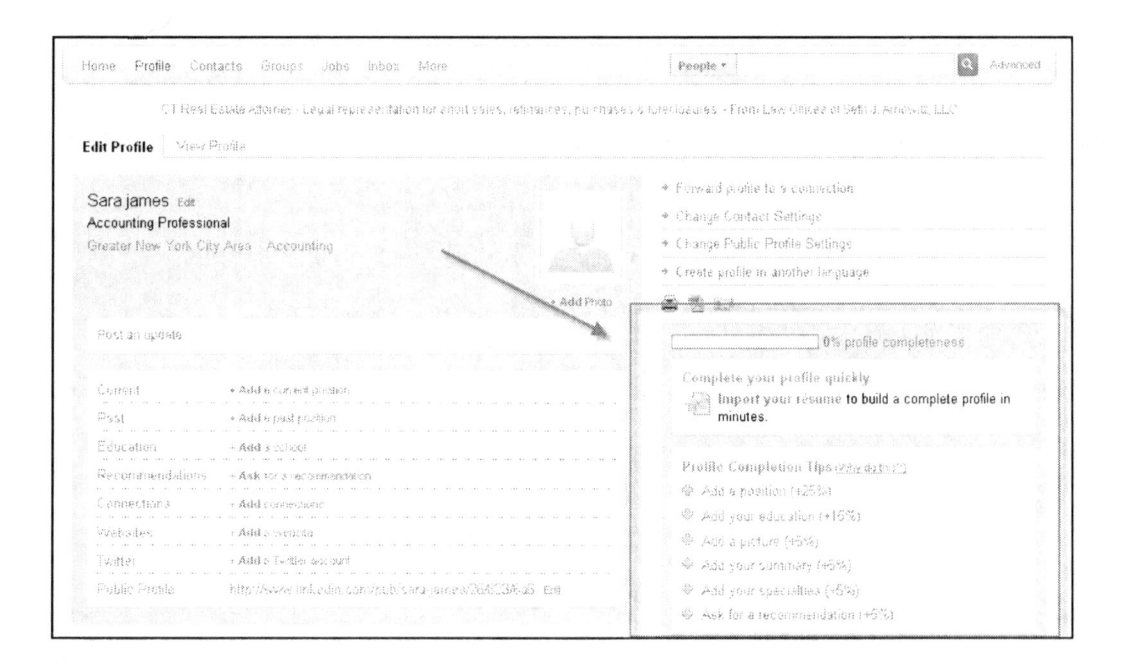

You can upload your resume if you would like to get started quickly and then go back and tweak the position titles. As you can see you get profile completeness points as you move through the tasks. Strive to have your profile

100% complete before you begin to connect.

Another area I would like to draw your attention to is the website area.

When you add your website(s) in the profile, instead of choosing the ready-made titles like Personal Website, Company Website, etc. click "other" from the drop down menu. The reason for this is you can then name the link whatever you want, including your keywords!

Instead of "Personal Website" which is what would come up if you clicked that option, you name your website title with your keywords.

Example:

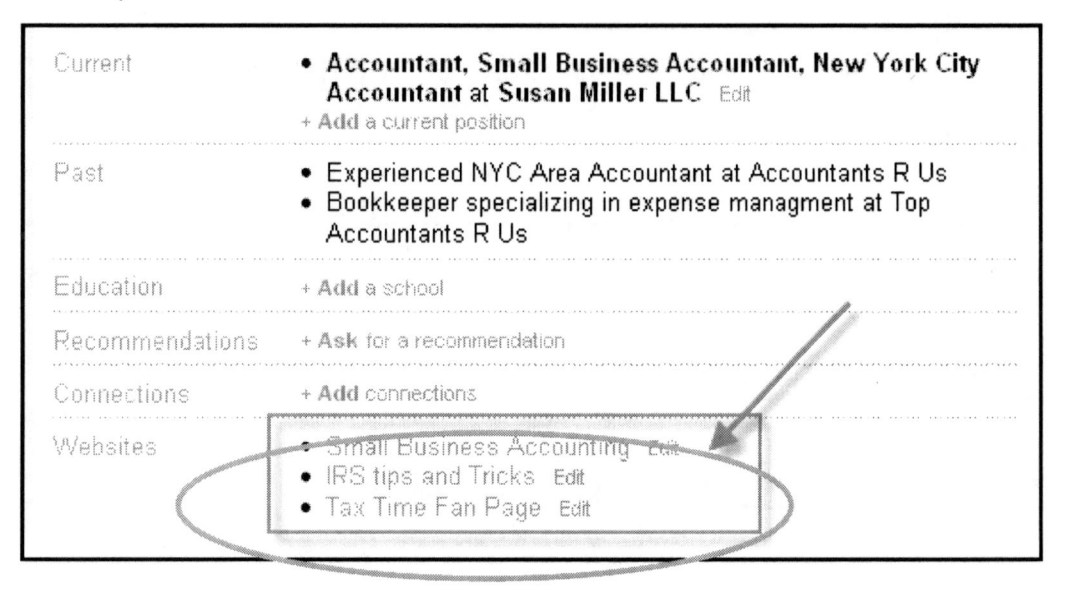

If you want to put a link to your blog in here, still use "other" and put whatever title you would like that is KEYWORD RICH.

Fill this out completely, even if you only have one website and no blog, use the same web address just different keywords. If you have a Facebook® personal profile or fan page, you may want to name one of the website links "Like us on Facebook".

Once you have completed this go back to the navigation bar and to the "edit page" link.

Next add your Twitter account:

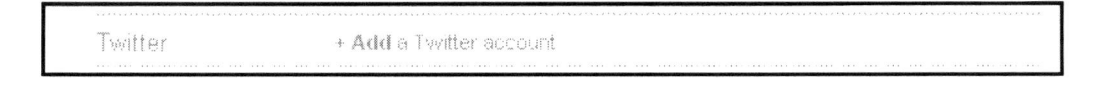

The last step would be to select a custom Linkedin URL. This is a great way for you to promote your presence on the network when you are off line. You can put this address on your business cards or email signature for easy connecting. Say something like: "Connect with me on LinkedIn" with your own URL.

If your profile is already active, you can change the URL address by going to the "edit profile" area or in the privacy settings screens. I recommend you use your name or some variation of your name. If your name is already being used by someone else on the platform, try and use your middle initial or full middle name. For me, I decided to use an abbreviation of my first name "Kat" for Kathryn, my first initial and then last name – katkrose. So my URL is http://linkedin.com/in/katkrose. Use whatever is comfortable for you.

Continue to set up your profile using the sections below the main window:

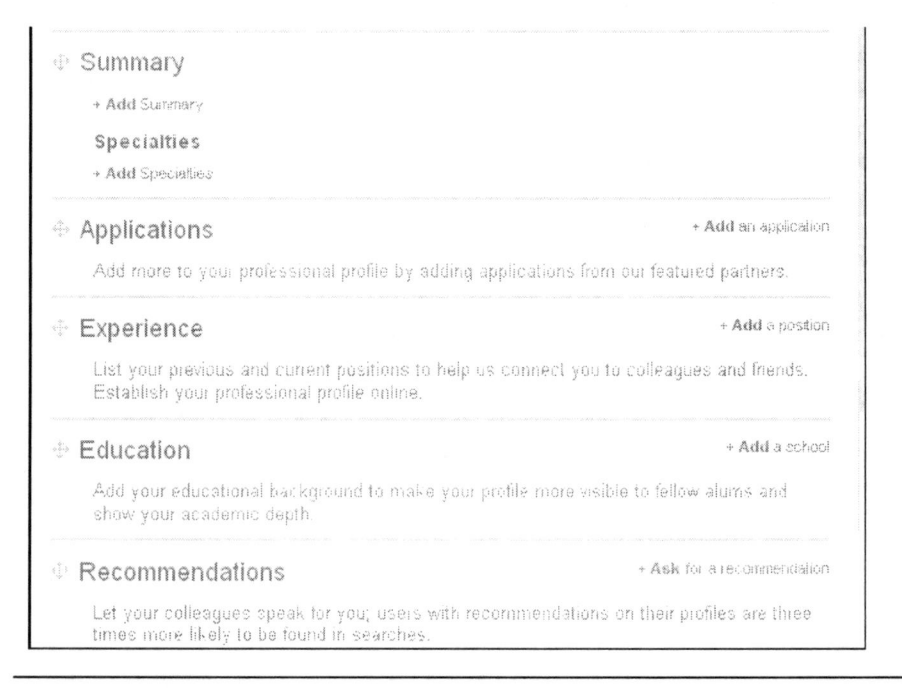

Begin with the Summary and Specialties section:

Summary [Edit]

None ✛ Add Summary

Specialties:
None ✛ Add Specialties

Make sure again this is keyword rich content that will allow people to find you in a search.

Summary [Edit]

Financial exec with broad experience in all aspects of accounting, auditing and financial management. Direct experience with real estate, financial consulting and venture capital. Interested in connecting with small to medium sized businesses that have financial management needs.

Specialties:
Accounting, Finance, Financial Planning, mergers and acquisitions

If you haven't already, use the appropriate "edit" links to add your past positions and, again, be mindful of the titles and descriptions to maximize keywords and searching capabilities.

Don't forget to add in the education section. This will help you begin to connect because based upon this information, Linkedin will suggest connections for you.

The next section toward the bottom of this page asks for your personal information. I never recommend you give any personal information away on social networks. It is simply not necessary. Linkedin gives prospects a way to contact you if they are interested in connecting. If you do decide to fill this information out, I will cover some privacy settings on the platform in the next chapter.

The next section is the contact settings. This area allows you let others who want to connect with you know why you are on Linkedin and what kind of networking opportunities you are interested in. It is my recommendation to check all the boxes, however, if you are currently employed, your employer may not be pleased to see that your profile lists you as "seeking career opportunities".

Contact Settings

Besides helping you find people and opportunities through your network, LinkedIn makes it easy for opportunities to find you. In deciding how other LinkedIn users may contact you, take care not to exclude contacts inadvertently that you might find professionally valuable.

What type of messages will you accept?

◉ I'll accept Introductions and InMail
○ I'll accept only Introductions

Opportunity Preferences

What kinds of opportunities would you like to receive?

☑ Career opportunities   ☑ Expertise requests
☑ Consulting offers   ☑ Business deals
☑ New ventures   ☑ Personal reference requests
☑ Job inquiries   ☑ Requests to reconnect

What advice would you give to users considering contacting you?

Include comments on your availability, types of projects or opportunities that interest you, and what information you'd like to see included in a request. To avoid unwanted contacts, **do not** include contact information, since your response will be visible to your entire network. See examples.

You can also offer "advice" to those who are considering contacting you. You may want to give some specific criteria and perhaps the best time of day/method to contact you.

The last area is the "applications" section.   I will cover adding applications later in this book so I recommend you skip it for now.

Chapter 5: Privacy Settings on Linkedin

Like any other social network, you will want to be aware of the privacy settings available on Linkedin. To access these settings, go to the upper right side of the screen and click on the drop down next to your name, then click on "settings":

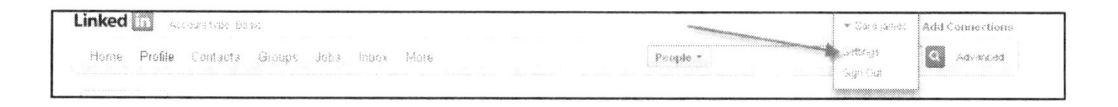

In this section you can configure all of your profile settings and personal information:

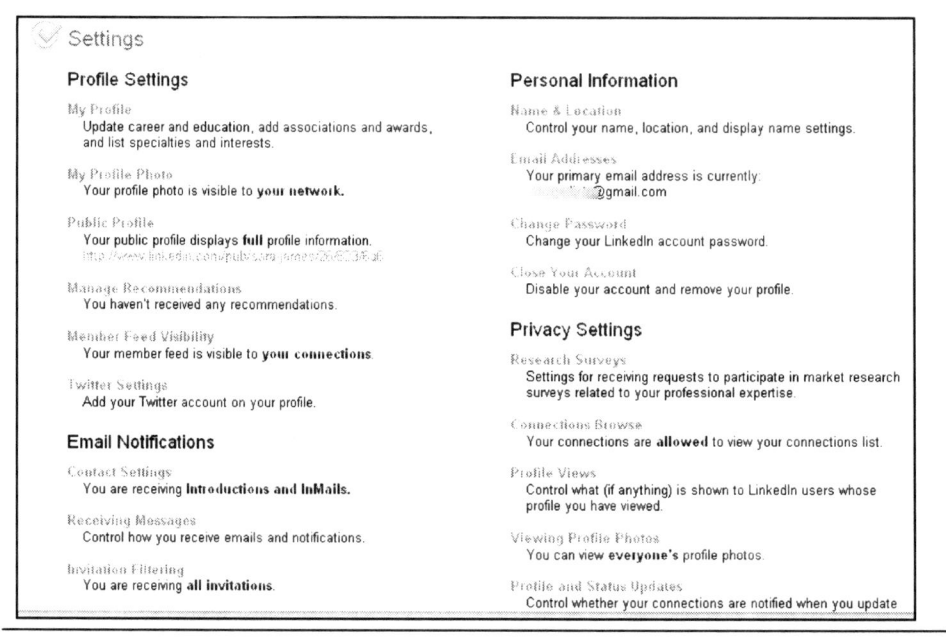

I recommend you take the time to go through this area and be sure your privacy settings are configured properly.

Most of these are self-explanatory but there are a few areas I would like to draw your attention to:

Public Profile:

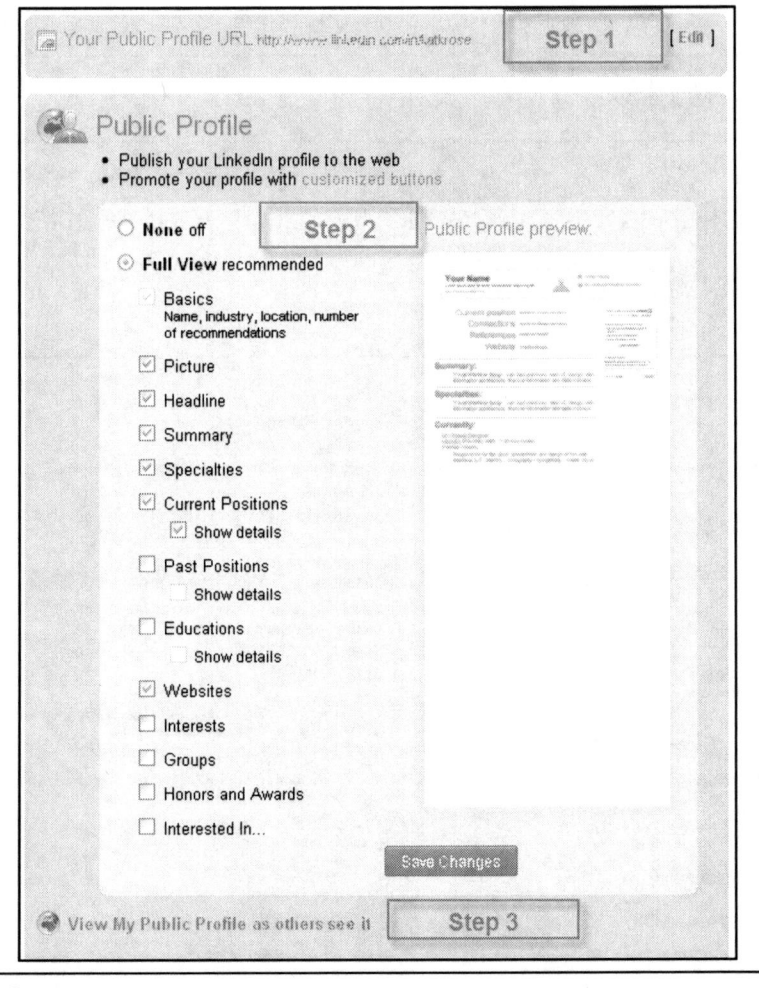

In the first step you can view or change your "Public Profile URL".

In the second step you want to verify that your public profile is published to the web. If the "none off" box is checked no one will be able to find you on the network.

Below there you can adjust the different types of information that are publicly available to anyone who is searching the internet. Your public profile is viewable by the general public if they happen to Google your name and your Linkedin profile comes up. I would like to point out however that your contact settings and personal information are NOT viewable outside of Linkedin.

The last step, step three, allows you to click and view how your profile looks to those who are viewing your public information. You can decide how much or how little information you share. On the right side in the box you can see a public profile preview window as well.

The last area on this screen is the "customized buttons" link.

I always recommend that you promote yourself both ON and OFF of all social networks. In this section you can download buttons for your blog, online resume, website or email signature. Simply copy the code provided and paste it in the appropriate area.

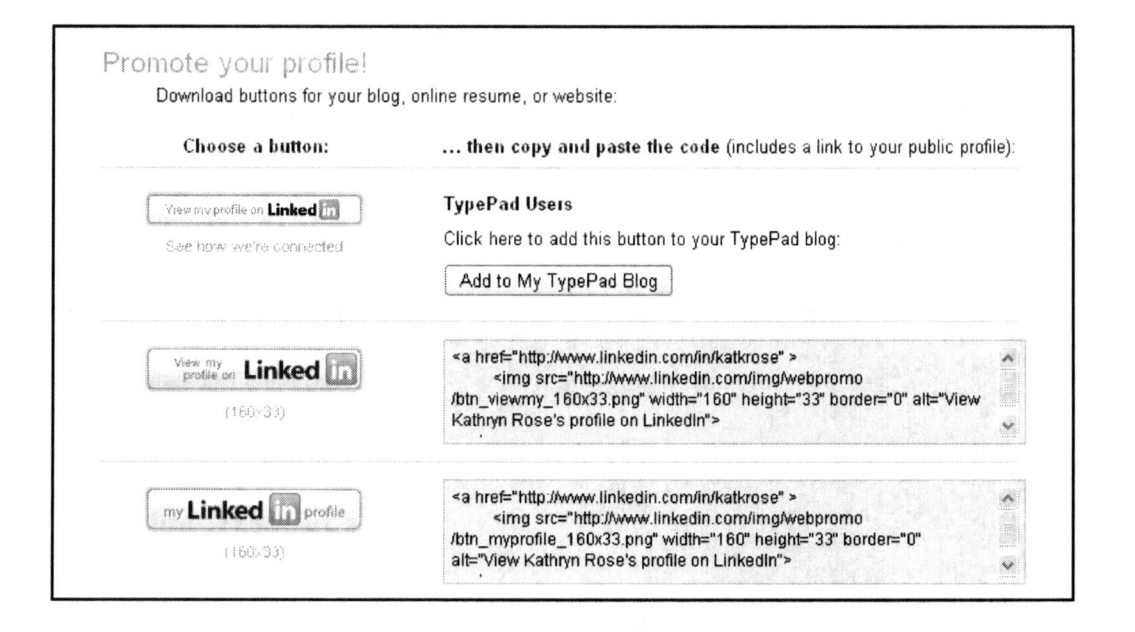

There are many different styles and sizes to choose from, select which ones complement your online properties.

The next area is the Email Notifications section:

Email Notifications

Contact Settings
You are receiving **Introductions and InMails.**

Receiving Messages
Control how you receive emails and notifications.

Contact Settings:

This setting controls how other Linkedin users contact you. I recommend accepting all introductions and "inmail" which is essentially a private message from another Linkedin user.

Contact Settings

Besides helping you find people and opportunities through your network, LinkedIn makes it easy for opportunities to find you. In deciding how other LinkedIn users may contact you, take care not to exclude contacts inadvertently that you might find professionally valuable.

What type of messages will you accept?

  ◉ I'll accept Introductions and InMail
  ○ I'll accept only Introductions

You also had access to this area on the "edit profile" screen.

Receiving Messages:

This is an area I highly recommend you review closely. You can get inundated with emails from the network particularly if you begin to connect with a great number of people and you join a significant number of groups. See the grid below:

Receiving Messages

LinkedIn will send you a notification when you receive important messages from other users. How would you like to receive these notifications?

	Individual Email	Daily Digest Email	Weekly Digest Email	No Email
	Send emails to me immediately.	Send one bundle per day.	Send one bundle email per week.	Read messages on the website
General				
InMails, Introductions, and OpenLink (?)	○	Not Available	◉	○
Invitations (?)	◉	Not Available	○	○
Profile Forwards (?)	◉	Not Available	○	○
Job Notifications (?)	◉	Not Available	○	○
Questions from your Connections (?)	◉	Not Available	○	○
Replies/Messages from connections (?)	◉	Not Available	○	○
Network Updates (?)	Not Available	Not Available	◉	○
Referral Center Messages (?)	Not Available	Not Available	◉	○
Discussions				
Network Update Activity (?)	◉	Not Available	Not Available	○
Groups				
Invitations to join groups (?)	◉	Not Available	○	○
Group Digest Emails (?)				

In fact, for most I recommend setting up a completely separate gmail or other type of email account specifically for your Linkedin emails. This way you can keep track of them easily and your main email inbox doesn't get filled with network messages.

The next area is Personal Information:

Personal Information

Name & Location
Control your name, location, and display name settings.

Email Addresses
Your primary email address is currently:
rosekathryn@sbcglobal.net

Name and location: You can change your name and location in this section. You have the preference here to choose how your name is displayed on the network.

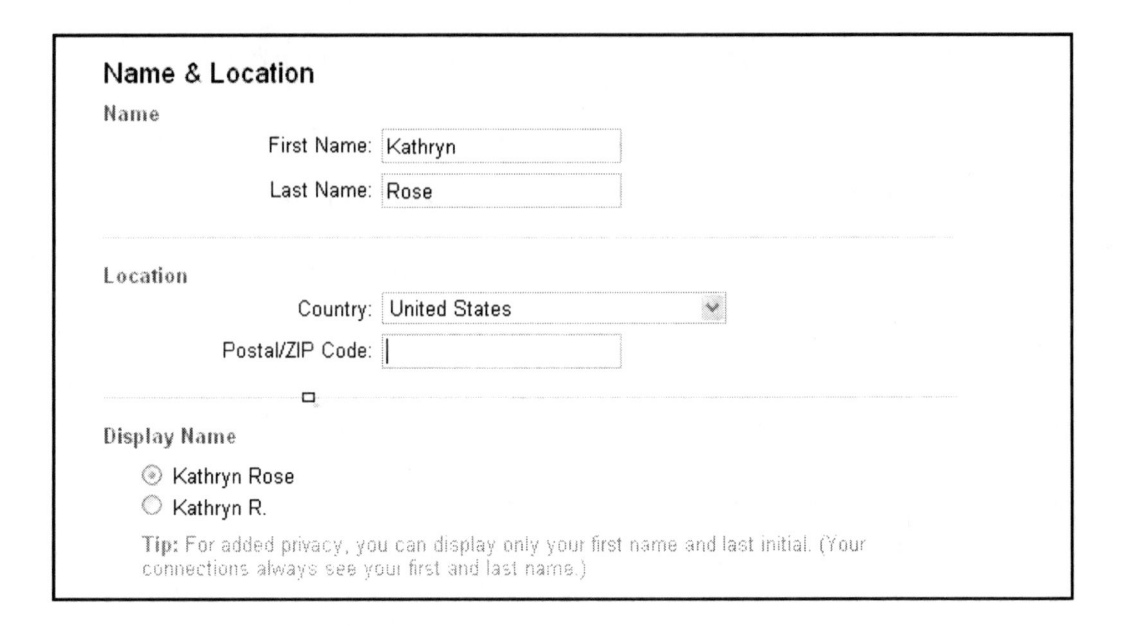

Email Address:

Here you will find the list of your active email addresses and you can set your primary address.

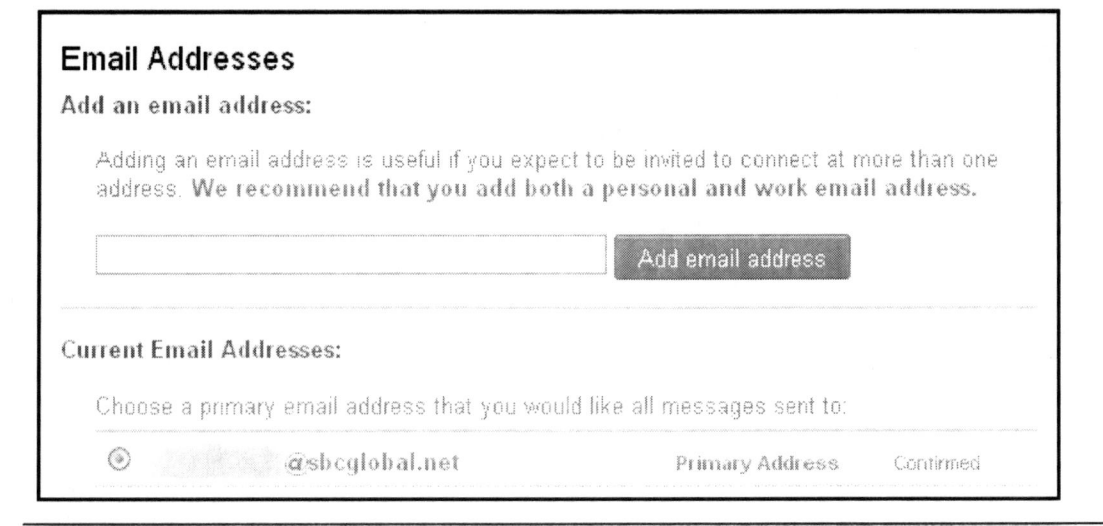

Next we move on to the Privacy Settings Area:

I will touch on a couple of areas here that I feel are the most important.

Privacy Settings

Research Surveys
   Settings for receiving requests to participate in market research surveys related to your professional expertise.

Connections Browse
   Your connections are **allowed** to view your connections list.

Profile Views
   Control what (if anything) is shown to LinkedIn users whose profile you have viewed.

Research Surveys:

This is a simple "yes/no" indicating your interest in becoming part of market research surveys.

Connections Browse:

This is a very important area particularly if you are connecting to current or past clients. You may wish to restrict access to your connections list so you don't inadvertently give your competition your client list.

Profile views:

When you view other Linkedin profiles, you may decide to let the person know you viewed it. This setting controls how your information is displayed to those whose profiles you have visited.

You can decide that you want others to see your entire name and headline, an anonymous profile characteristic summary or nothing.

For example, on your homepage you will see this on the right side:

If you want to see who has viewed your profile, you must allow others to see that you have visited theirs.

This can be a very powerful tool particularly if you are in sales or looking to connect with specific people on the network. You can see if your profile is being viewed by those in your target market and perhaps drop them a note or a connection request to follow up.

Chapter 6: Creating Connections

The most obvious way to start creating connections is by inviting people who already know you. When sending out connection invitations be sure to write a **PERSONAL** note, not the standard, "I'd like you to join my LinkedIn network". Even if you know the person, it is good to get in the habit of doing this so you'll be more likely to continue the practice with others.

Try something like:

> ➤ "We worked together at ABC company and I look forward to reconnecting. . ."
>
> ➤ "I have been to many of your seminars and workshops and would like to add you to my professional network"
>
> ➤ "I'm looking to expand my professional network with professionals in the same industry, it would be great to connect with you here . . ."
>
> ➤ "We are connected on Facebook (Twitter, etc.) and I wanted to connect here also"

➤ "I am a long time subscriber to your newsletter and would be honored to connect here."

Finding Connections on Linkedin

Remember that Linkedin, unlike many other social networks is a PROFESSIONAL connection space. There are different ways to find connections:

➤ **You can enter their email address**
➤ **Type their name in the "search" bar at the top**
➤ **Look for current and past colleagues by clicking on a company**
➤ **Look for classmates by clicking on a school**
➤ **Joining Groups**

Using the search feature on Linkedin to find connections:

As I mentioned above, you can go to the top of the page and simply type the person's name in the search area and a list of people will come up. You can then most likely find the person you want to connect with by their photo, company or other identifying characteristics.

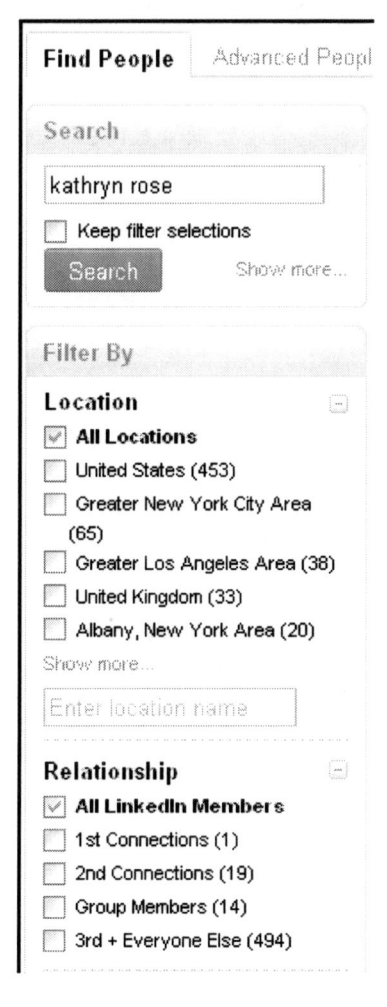

If you don't see the person on the first page, you can go onto the left side of the screen and filter your results by location, relationship, etc.

Once you find the individual you would like to connect with you click "add to network" and the box on the following page will appear.

You must be careful to only invite those you actually know to connect. If too many people label you a "spammer" i.e. select the "I don't know this person" when declining your invitation, your account can and will be shut down.

I have other tips for connecting later in this book.

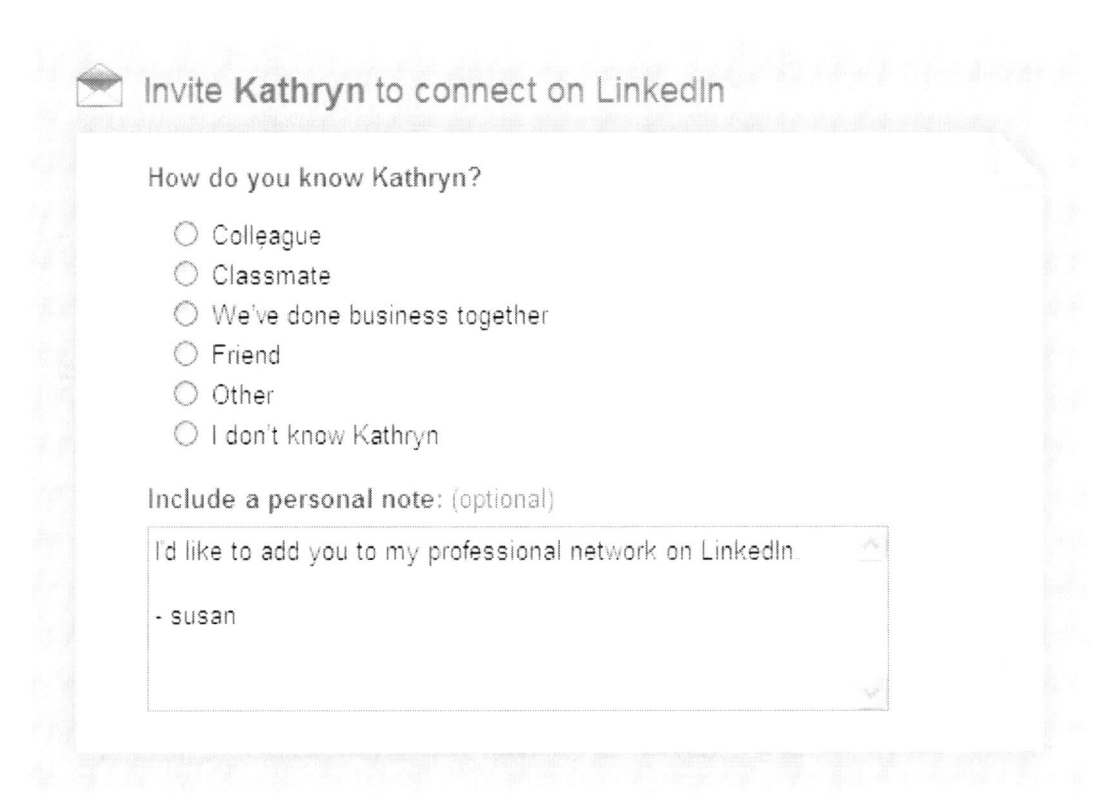

When you click the appropriate category, Linkedin may ask you to identify the company or the college to make sure that you are only inviting people you know. This information is taken from your own entries into your profile. For example if you say your past position was with XYZ

Company, when you select "colleague" or "We've done business together, you will be asked to select which company so you will select XYZ Company. If you click "friend" you will most likely be asked to enter their email address.

When someone confirms your request, they are added to your network and put in your connections list. These would be 1st degree connections. There are different levels of connections 1st, 2nd and 3rd. One of the true powers of LinkedIn is its 2nd and 3rd degree connections. This feature can give you literally a network of millions of people.

Here is a brief explanation of the different degrees of connections.

First-degree connections are people that you know personally; they have a direct relationship with you from their account to your account.

Second-degree network members are made up of people who know at least one member of your first-degree network connections; the friends of your friends. You can reach any of your second-degree network members by your first-degree connection to introduce you to his or her friend.

Third-degree network members are made up of people who know at least one of your second-degree network members; in other words; the friends of your friends of your friends. You can reach any of your third-degree network members by asking your friend to pass along an introduction from you to his or her friend, who then passes it to his or her friend, who is a third-degree member.

How powerful can these connections be? Three degrees of separation can give you access to a network of millions of people.

It is easier to connect up with people who are in your network, even if they are a third degree rather than if they are "outside your network."

Advanced Search

If you want to be more thorough when finding people to connect with or are searching for a specific targeted list of prospects or candidates, you can use the "advanced" search setting.

Go to the top right of the page and click on the "advanced" link next to the magnifying glass:

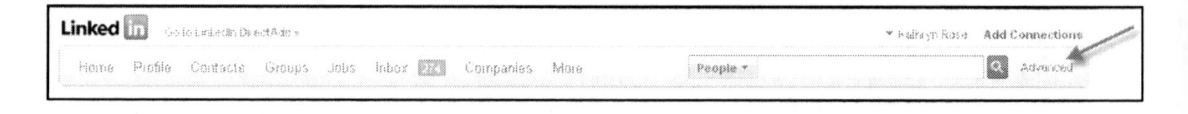

Once you do you will come to this screen:

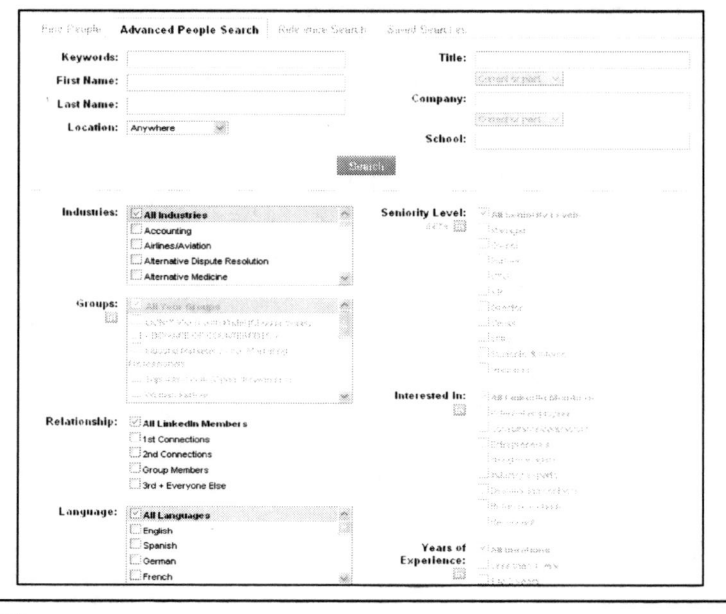

This is a great way to find out who in your target market is on the network. You can use keywords, the person's name, title, etc. You can also look across locations, industries or languages and more. If you are a premium member more options are available to you to find your next prospect, business partner and so on.

The next tab in this section is the "reference search" area. This is a little known search tool in the platform. This allows you to search for anyone who might be able to provide you with a reference for a potential employee or business partner.

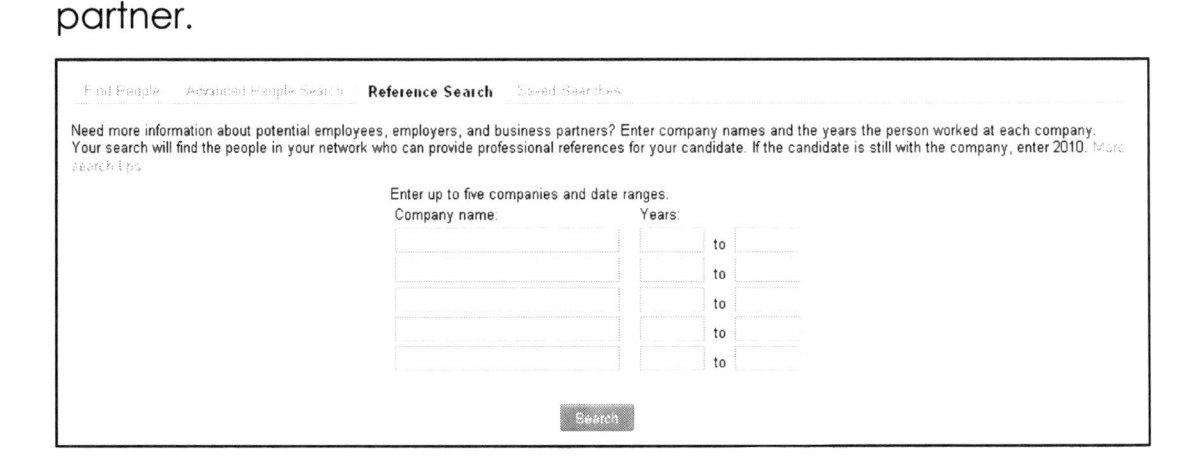

Simply put the company name in the box and the years in which the potential candidate worked at the company.

Enter up to five companies and date ranges.

Company name: Years:

Credit Suisse	2001	to	2006
		to	
		to	
		to	
		to	

Search

Click search and you will see how many of your connections meet that criteria and possibly can provide a reference for that person:

Your reference search found **856** people:

   9 are your connections

   847 are friends of your connections

... who worked with your candidate at this company:

   Credit Suisse

You can get a list of those potential references and contact them directly via InMail™ when you upgrade to a Business or Pro account.

Upgrade now

As you can see above, you would need a paid account to get a list of these people and be able to contact them directly. However, if you do not have a paid account you can simply go back to the advanced search screen, type in the company name and find out who those 9 first degree connections are. I highly recommend upgrading if you are doing a great deal of hiring or need additional references for other types of business associates.

Chapter 7: Managing Introductions

How can I get introduced to people outside my network?

Just like when you are networking in person; you ask for permission. Often times I email the connector outside Linkedin and ask for an introduction. You should definitely make it clear WHY you want to be connected so the connector can determine that this is a legitimate request. I'm sure you're protective of your contacts, you just don't go around handing out your contact list -- it's the same with others you are asking to introduce you.

Linkedin has a great help area that answers this question:

How can I request an Introduction to someone I am not currently connected to?

Introductions let you contact users in your network who are two or three degrees away from you. You can send an Introduction request through the connections you know and trust. Your connection (at their discretion) can then forward the Introduction request on to the desired recipient. To get introduced take the following actions:

Locate the member's Linkedin Profile.

Click on 'Get introduced'. To be able to utilize the Introduction feature, the person you are attempting to reach must be either a 2nd or 3rd Degree connection.

If this is the case, the 'Get introduced...' link will be visible on the right area of their LinkedIn Profile.

If more than one of your connections are also connected to this person you will have to select one of them from a list of connections available to introduce you. Fill out the information requested.

Request an Introduction

To: Kathryn Rose

From: Susan Miller

☑ Include my contact information

Enter the contact information you would like to share

Email: susanmiller@gmx.com

Phone: [   ]

Category: [Choose...   ▼]

Subject: [   ]

Your message to Kathryn:

[   ]

Kathryn is interested in: consulting offers, new ventures, job inquiries, expertise requests, business deals, reference requests, getting back in touch

Kathryn's contact advice:

By default, the message is set to 'include my contact information'. If you do not wish to share contact information at this time, click on this box until the check mark no longer appears.

Select a 'Category' from the dropdown menu. Reasons to be used for an Introduction could be to discuss:

- ➢ **A career opportunity.**
- ➢ **A consulting offer.**
- ➢ **A new venture.**
- ➢ **A job Inquiry.**
- ➢ **An expertise request.**
- ➢ **A business deal.**
- ➢ **A reference request.**
- ➢ **An opportunity to get back in touch.**

Prior to selecting a reason listed above, **review the area to the right** of the message text box to identify what the member is interested in when being contacted through this feature.

Linkedin asks that you be respectful of the member's wishes and only use an Introduction Request if the category chosen falls in to what is listed in their interests. For example do not send an introduction request for a career opportunity to someone who identifies that they are only interested in getting back in touch with old contacts. Members not abiding by this may be negatively perceived as a spammer by that person.

Type a message to the person you are requesting to be introduced to. Then type a brief note to the person who will forward the introduction.

Click on the 'Send' button.

How do I increase my chances that the person will forward the connection?

You need to make it clear why you are asking for the introduction. As I mentioned earlier, just like when you are networking in person you want to ask the connection what they think the person would be interested in hearing or learning about you so they will feel comfortable connecting to you.

There is no rule that a connection HAS to forward your request so it's best to ask for connections through people you know well. Not to say that you should not try and connect through others, just that you may not be a successful. Perhaps a good strategy would be to try and form a better relationship with the connection before asking for their introductions.

When writing your message to your intended recipient, keep these tips in mind to increase your chances in reaching a positive outcome:

- ➢ **Be honest and upfront**
- ➢ **Be succinct**
- ➢ **Be original**
- ➢ **Be ready to give in order to get**

Managing Introduction Requests

What if someone in your network is looking for your assistance to meet someone in your network?

Now that your reputation is on the line too, you need to be strategic about processing any introduction requests that come your way. You really have only two options for handling an Introduction request:

> **Accept it and forward it on to the party it's intended for (we recommend that you compose a message to accompany the introduction request prior to sending it to the intended recipient)**
> **Decline it politely**

How do I gracefully decline requests?

There may come a point when you receive an Introduction Request that you simply don't feel comfortable sending on; maybe you don't know the contact who made the request well enough (or know enough about that person). Perhaps you're unclear about that person's true motives or objectives, or maybe your relationship with the recipient isn't at the level where you feel you can facilitate an introduction. Don't ever feel pressured to forward an Introduction Request and if you're uncomfortable, the best response is simply to decline the request and describe why you're declining to forward the request.

Here are some tips on how to respond:

- **Simply inform the initial contact that you're not that deeply connected with the intended recipient**
- **Let the requesting party know that the recipient doesn't respond well to this approach**
- **You think that their request needs work – you're vouching for that person so you don't want to pass along a shoddy or questionable request that could reflect badly on you.**

Connecting Through Groups

A much faster and easier way to connect with people outside your network and without having to ask for introductions is to join a Linkedin Group. Most group settings are configured so if you are a member of a group that will also be a connection option:

I will cover Groups later in this book but this is a great way to connect with prospects—joining groups they are a part of. As I mentioned above, this way you don't need their email address or ask a connection to refer you.

Connections through outside networks

Once you become a regular user on the network, you may see people identify themselves as LION's or TOP Linked networkers. LION stands for Linkedin Open Networker and TopLinked is a service that connects people on Linkedin who are open to receiving connection requests from anyone who pays for the service. In other words, you are an OPEN networker meaning that once you join the group or identify yourself as such, you are letting people know that you will almost always accept a connection request. Why "almost" always? I am an open networker but I have been contacted to connect by profiles that just seem fake to me. There are a lot of spammers so you need to be careful. The biggest difference with open networkers is you agree that you won't label someone as a "spammer" by saying "I don't know this person" when they try to connect with you. You will simply ignore the request.

If you are someone who would like to grow their network quickly I recommend joining an open networker type group like Toplinked.

TopLinked.com

TopLinked.com is THE secret of how to build larger, more diverse, and more valuable networks on the world's top social networking sites.

TopLinked people are people like you - people who know the incredible value of being open to new opportunities and new connections.

They are the most helpful and connected people on any social networking site.

TopLinked.com is THE quick and easy way to get connected with ALL of them!

TopLinked.com has been helping people grow larger, more diverse, and more valuable networks since 2006.

And through a shared backend database with our sister site OpenNetworker.com, you can also grow your networks on 20+ other social networking sites (when you join TopLinked.com, it is the same as joining OpenNetworker.com and visa versa)

There is a TopLinked Invite Me List for every top social networking site: LinkedIn, Facebook, Twitter, MySpace, Ecademy, Xing, Bebo, Blue Chip Expert, Fast Pitch, Friendster, hi5, Konnects, Affluence.org, Naymz, Orkut, Perfect Networker, Plaxo, Ryze, Tagged, UNYK and Viadeo.

As a TopLinked.com Member you can add yourself to any (or all) of those Lists and be invited by your fellow Open Networkers to connect (and/or use those Lists to invite them)

Start accelerating the growth of your networks and opportunities

Click Here to Sign Up!

TopLinked.com Home Page
About TopLinked.com
Happy TopLinked Members

TopLinked.com Top 50 List
TopLinked.com Top Supporters

Add Yourself to the Invite Me List
Add Yourself to the Top Supporter List

TopLinked.com Account
Contact TopLinked.com

Chapter 8: Beginning the Conversation

In addition to optimizing your profile, you want to make sure you're using all of the benefits of Linkedin to let your connections and potential connections know what you and your company are about. One of the ways to do this is the "Share an update" area on the homepage:

This area is a type of status update. Before you write something in here, remember: Linkedin is a PROFESSIONAL network. This isn't the place to talk about what movie you're seeing tonight.

Use this space to announce new products, services or clients or projects you are working on. You may also share article excerpts, blog posts, information about your industry or other relevant content.

You can have control over who can see what you're sharing by clicking on the drop down area next to the post:

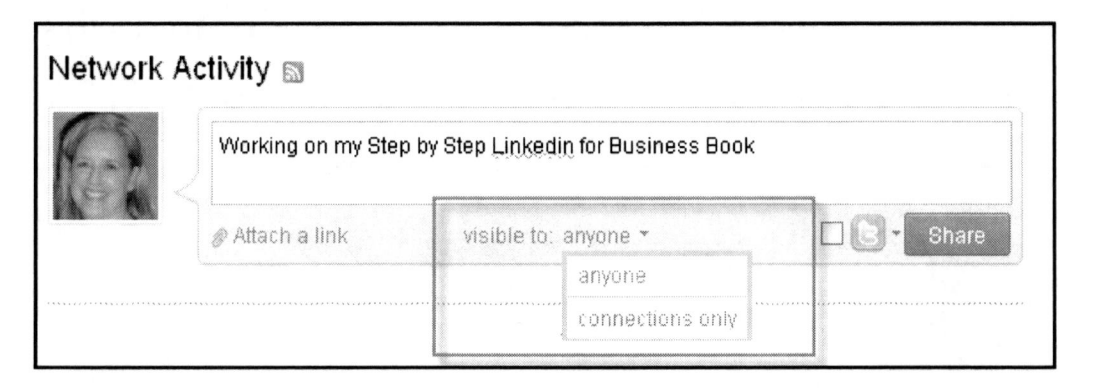

You can decide whether it's everyone who views your page or only your connections.

You can even share articles with your connections:

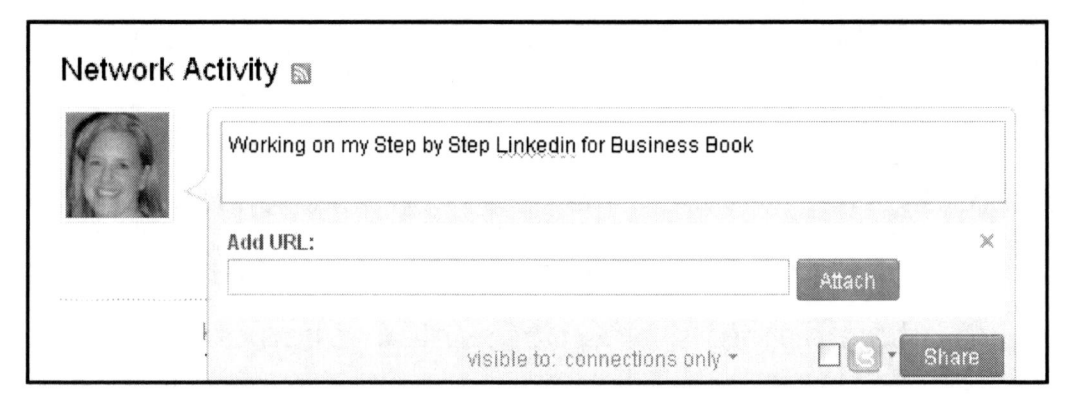

Chapter 9: Grow Your Sphere Of Influence Through Linkedin Groups

As I mentioned earlier, one of the reasons to join groups is because it makes it easier to connect with your target audience on Linkedin. When you click on the person's name and click "add to network" you can say you know the person through a group and bypass the need to have their personal email or ask another person to introduce you.

There are other reasons to join Linkedin Groups. They are are a great way to connect to like minded individuals and establish yourself as an expert in your field.

There are different ways to connect through Linkedin Groups. You can start your own group on a subject or join one already in existence. Some groups require approval, others do not. To find groups go to the search bar and click the drop down box and select "search groups." Type in your category and look at the different groups that are available to join.

How do I get the most out of joining a group?

- ➢ **Post questions and make high quality posts with great content**
- ➢ **Gain connections through groups, invite others in group to connect**
- ➢ **Comment and answer on other's questions, establish yourself as an expert**

Tip: look for groups that have a robust membership and have recent activities and discussions. There is no point in joining groups that are not active.

Also, do not join a group with the intent to post promotional messages. Most groups now have a promotional message filter and your posts will be placed there if another member flags your content as promotional. Do it too often and you can be removed from the group.

Create your own Linkedin Group:

I recommend that until you get comfortable interacting, connecting and sharing on the network you just become a member of groups before starting your own. Many people go ahead and start a group without realizing that it takes strategy, focus and time to grow and maintain a successful Linkedin group. Once you get started searching groups you will see many that do not have any activity or are full of spammy promotional messages because someone thought it was a good idea to start a group but did not want to put the time into growing and maintaining it.

Here are the steps to start a group:

1. Think about the objective of the group. Are you trying to position yourself as an expert? Gain contacts and prospects? Offer information? Write down your objectives.

2. Decide if you have the time to manage a group. Groups only thrive when they are constantly fed content, moderated and interacted with by the group creator(s). If you leave the group alone too long, it will become a free-for all and you will not be able to achieve your objectives.

3. Decide what your group will be about. Check to see what other competitive groups are already present on Linkedin and see what they are doing to interact with their members. Just because someone already has a group in your niche, does not mean there is not room for another. You may just have to come up with a different "spin" on the topic to attract quality members.

To start a group on Linkedin:

First go to the "Groups" dropdown and select "Create a Group."

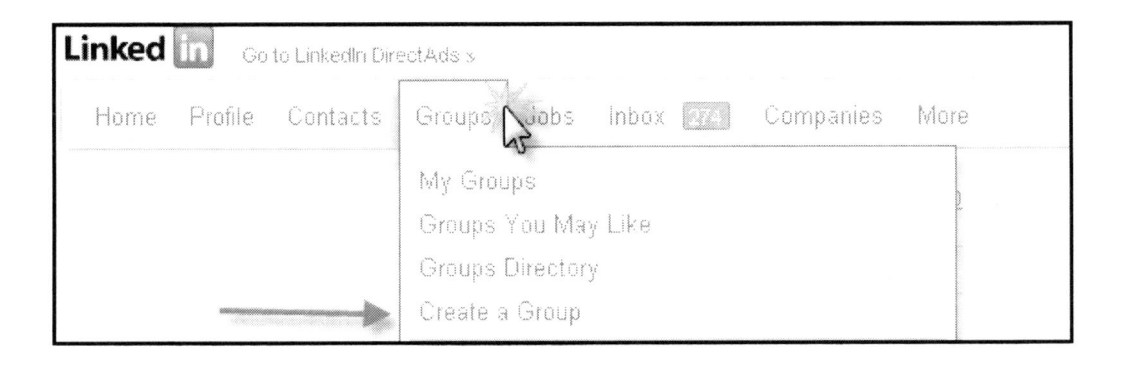

On the next screen you will be asked to upload a logo and I recommend you create one that will represent your group in the best light. These are professional groups and can grow to hundreds of thousands of members. It is best to have an identity in mind.

You will also be asked to fill in information about your group:

Home   Profile   Contacts   Groups   Jobs   Inbox ▨   Companies   More   Groups ▼

My Groups   Following   Groups You May Like   Groups Directory   **Create a Group**   F

Logo: Your logo will appear in the Groups Directory and on your group pages.

[_____] [Browse...]

Note: PNG, JPEG, or GIF only, max size 100 KB.

☐ * I acknowledge and agree that the logo/image I am uploading does not infringe upon any third party copyrights, trademarks, or other proprietary rights or otherwise violate the User Agreement.

* Group Name: [_____]

Note: "LinkedIn" is not allowed to be used in your group name.

* Group Type: [Choose . ▼]

* Summary: Enter a brief description about your group and its purpose. Your summary about this group will appear in the Groups Directory.

[_____]

* Description: Your full description of this group will appear on your group pages.

[_____]

Website: [_____]

* Group Owner Email: [_____]

* Access: ○ Open Access: Any LinkedIn member may join this group without requiring approval from a manager.
                       ◉ Request to Join: Users must request to join this group and be approved by a manager.

                       ☑ Display this group in the Groups Directory.
                       ☑ Allow members to display the logo on their profiles. Also, send my connections a Network Update that I have created this group.
                       ☐ Allow members to invite others to join this group.
                       Pre-approve members with the following email domain(s):

[_____]

Language: [English ▼]

Location: ☐ My group is based in a single geographic location.

* Agreement: ☐ Check to confirm you have read and accept the Terms of Service

[Create Group] or Cancel

Use the information from the questions you answered at the beginning of this section as a guide for filling out the Summary and Description area.

A couple of items to focus on:

Group type

Because there are a lot of reasons to create a group, LinkedIn has established the following six primary categories of groups:

- Alumni: These groups are alumni associations created by schools, or teaching institutions as a means to keep in touch with past graduates.

- Corporate: Corporate groups allow past and present employees from a single employer to stay in touch.

- Conference: As conference attendees plan to attend a particular conference, using a conference group to network with attendees ahead of time, during, and after the conference can be very advantageous. If the conference is a yearly event, the conference group would become a constant area of discussion, networking and planning.

- Networking: Coming together and meet similarly minded people who have a common interest can be fun and productive. Networking groups are organized around concepts like angel investors, women's networks, industry expertise, forums... These LinkedIn groups allow you to stay involved in your interests and meet people with similar or complementary goals.

- Non-Profit: These groups make it easier for volunteers to organize, plan, and execute projects and events relating to their charity without being in the same room – hence increasing their reach.

- Professional: Professional groups allow to network

with people in the same type of work or industry who are probably experiencing the same issues, problems, and potential solutions as you. These groups are often invaluable to further your career by giving you access to tips and strategies about your line of work and news about your industry.

Access:

Do you want your group open or do the potential participants need to be approved before they join?

○ **Open Access:** Any LinkedIn member may join this group without requiring approval from a manager.
◉ **Request to Join:** Users must request to join this group and be approved by a manager.

    ☑ Display this group in the Groups Directory.
    ☑ Allow members to display the logo on their profiles. Also, send my connections a Network Update that I have created this group.
    ☐ Allow members to invite others to join this group.
    Pre-approve members with the following email domain(s):

Again, groups are a great way to build your credibility but if you decide to start your own just be prepared to spend the time it takes providing good content and moderating the discussion.

Chapter 10: Adding Applications

Another way for connections and potential connections to get a "window" into you and your organization is by adding some applications.

Go to the top of your profile page or home page and click on my applications or get more applications:

This is a great feature because you can bring in additional resources to your page through these applications that will help people get to know you, your business or your services. Here are my recommended applications (some descriptions provided by LinkedIn applications pages):

Polls by LinkedIn

The **Polls** application is a market research tool that allows you to collect actionable data from your connections and the professional audience on LinkedIn.

Reading List by Amazon

Extend your professional profile by sharing the books you're reading with other LinkedIn members. Find out what you should be reading by following updates from your connections, people in your field, or other LinkedIn members of professional interest to you.

Projects and Teamspaces by Manymoon

Manymoon makes it simple to Get Work Done with your LinkedIn connections. Share and track unlimited tasks, projects, documents and Google Apps - for free!

Box.net Files by Box.net

Add the Box.net Files application to manage all your important files online. Box.net lets you share content on your profile, and collaborate with friends and colleagues.

Blog Link by SixApart

With **Blog Link**, you can get the most of your LinkedIn relationships by connecting your blog to your LinkedIn profile. Blog Link helps you, and your professional network, stay connected.

If you have a Wordpress blog I recommend this application:

WordPress by WordPress

Connect your virtual lives with the WordPress LinkedIn Application. With the WordPress App, you can sync your WordPress blog posts with your LinkedIn profile, keeping everyone you know in the know.

Company Buzz by LinkedIn

Ever wonder what people are saying about your company? **Company Buzz** shows you the Twitter activity associated with your company. View tweets, trends and top key words. Customize your topics and share with your coworkers.

Every second thousands of people are sending out messages about topics and companies through twitter. Company Buzz lets you tap into this information flow to find relevant trends and comments about your company. Install the application and instantly see what people are saying.

- ➤ Customize: **Modify the topics and add new ones to watch**
- ➤ Historical Data: **See historical charts to track buzz over time**
- ➤ Trends: **Get the top words associated with your topic and quickly drill into see related tweets**

Another Twitter related app is:

Tweets by LinkedIn

Access the most important parts of the professional conversation with Tweets, a Twitter client you can use right on LinkedIn. With Tweets, you can now display your most recent tweets on your LinkedIn profile. Tweets also gives you instant access to the updates of people you are following on Twitter and the power to tweet, reply, and re-tweet — all from your LinkedIn home page.

Events by LinkedIn

Announce and invite your connections to events, find professional events, from conferences to local meet-ups, and discover what events your connections are attending. I cover inviting connections to events in the next chapter.

SlideShare Presentations by SlideShare Inc

Slideshare- SlideShare is the world's largest community for sharing presentations. You can:

- **share presentations & documents with your LinkedIn network**
- **upload portfolios, resume, conference talks, PDFs, marketing/sales presentations etc**
- **display them on your LinkedIn profile**
- **all formats supported: ppt, pps, pptx, odp, pdf, doc, docx, odt, Keynote, iWork pages**
- **embed YouTube videos in presentations, add audio to make a webinar**

If you have a SlideShare.net account, you can import your existing presentations into LinkedIn. If you don't have one, signup from LinkedIn to share your presentations worldwide and get more views/traffic. This and the "google presentation" app below can be used to upload videos to your Linkedin profile.

Google Presentation by Google

Present yourself and your work. Upload a .PPT or use Google's online application to embed a presentation on your profile. You can also use this to upload videos to your Linkedin Profile.

Specialty applications:

Lawyer Ratings by LexisNexis Martindale-Hubbell

Are you a Legal Professional? Showcase your Martindale-Hubbell® Peer Review Ratings™ and Client Review Ratings™ to further validate your stated credentials and help you make the right connections.

FT Press Delivers by FT Press

FT Press Delivers provides essential insights for your business and career from today's leading business minds.

My Travel by TripIt, Inc. – **IMPORTANT NOTE**

Nothing says "Come and burglarize my home" like actually letting people know through apps like this that you are not at home. I cannot believe how many of my connections actually say they are out of town on a public network! The premise of this app is innocuous enough "See where your LinkedIn network is traveling and when you will be in the same city as your colleagues. Share your upcoming trips, current location, and travel stats with your network." But in reality it is a dangerous practice to announce your departure on any social network.

Huddle Workspaces by Huddle.net

Huddle gives you private, secure online workspaces packed with simple yet powerful project, collaboration and sharing tools for working with your connections.

SAP Community Bio by LinkedIn

Display your certified SAP expertise on LinkedIn. The **SAP Community Bio** application allows you to add your SAP contributions and credentials to your professional profile.

Legal Updates by JD Supra

Get legal news that matters to you and your business. (Lawyers, upload your articles and other content. Be found for your expertise on LinkedIn.)

Portfolio Display by Behance

Showcase your creative work in your LinkedIn Profile with the **Creative Portfolio Display** application. Free, easy to manage, and supports unlimited multimedia content.

  Real Estate Pro by Rofo

Access your local real estate and office space market. Follow active brokers, agents and professionals. Track new property listings and available spaces and stay informed of completed deals in your area.

Chapter 11: Linkedin Events

If you are having any kind of event either in person or virtual, using the Linkedin Events application helps you get the word out easily. I personally use this application a great deal and have seen very positive results.

To add an event to Linkedin go to the top left bar and click "more":

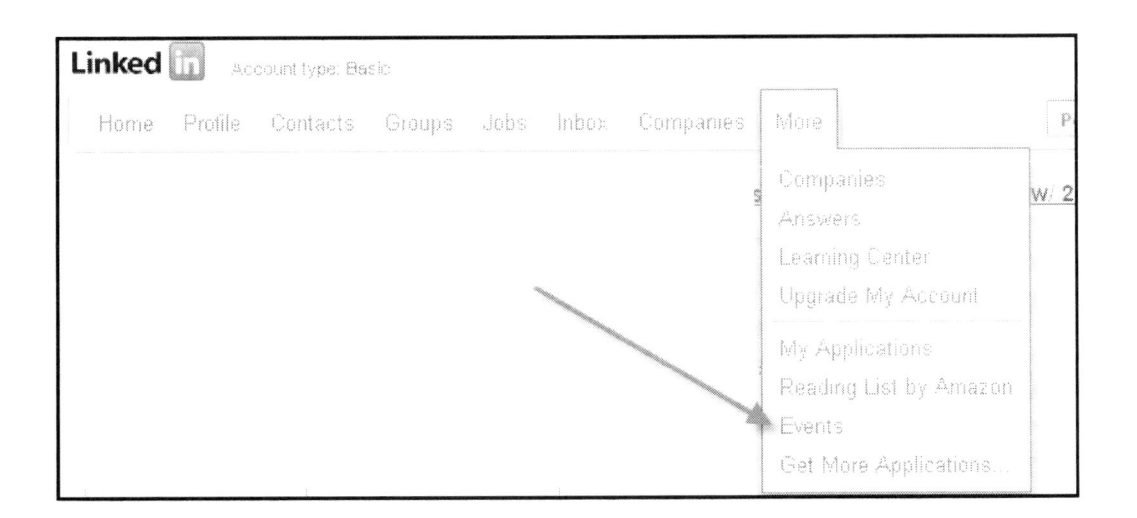

Then click on "Events", add an event:

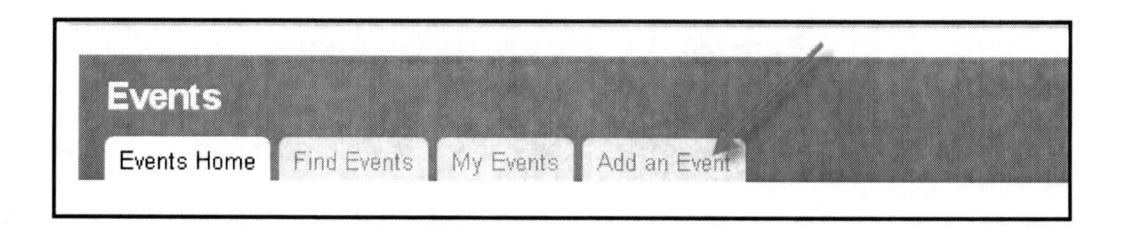

On the next screen you will add all the details of your event:

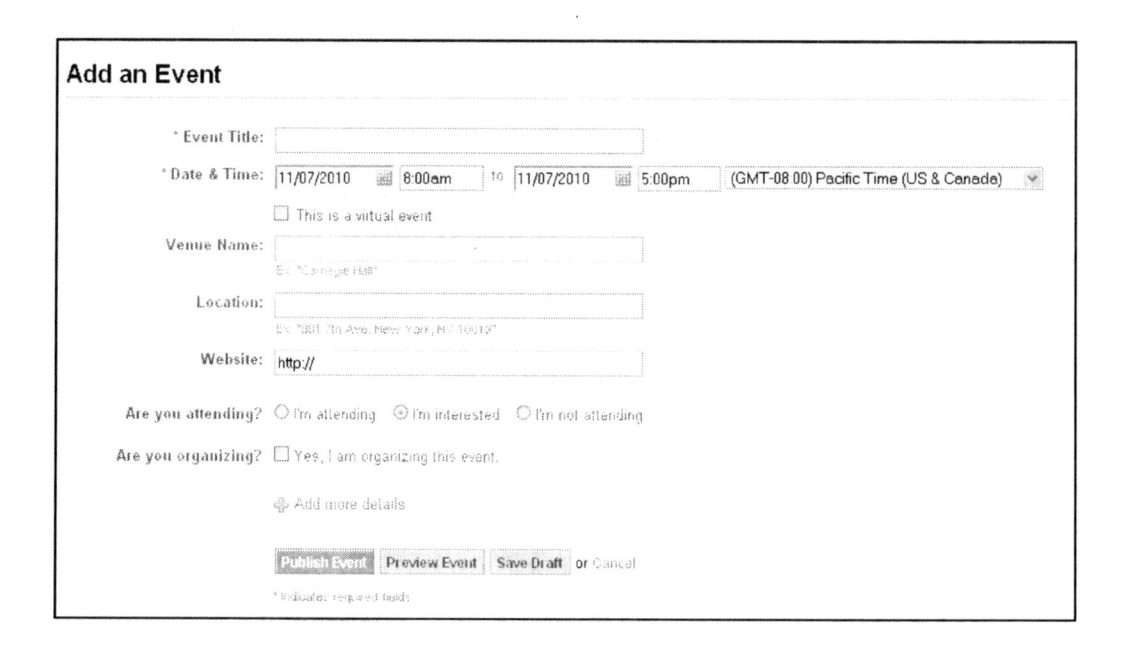

Fill in all the basic information and then click on "add more details"

On this screen you can add in a particulars about

---

the event, a descriptive paragraph, and so on.

Description: The event description will be displayed on the event page. The first 300 characters will be displayed to people browsing events. (No HTML)

Event Categorization

Event Type: Choose...

Industry: Choose...

Keywords: Keywords (also known as "tags") are descriptive words used to help people find events based on what the event is about. You may add up to 20 keywords.

Tip: Add multiple keywords by putting a comma after each

Who should attend? Tell us what types of people should attend your event by entering job titles. You may add up to 20 job titles.

Tip: Add multiple job titles by putting a comma after each

Event Organization

Are you attending? ○ I'm attending   ⊙ I'm interested   ○ I'm not attending

Are you organizing? ☐ Yes, I am organizing this event.

[Publish Event] [Preview Event] [Save Draft] or Cancel

* Indicates required fields

Once you finish the event, click "publish," an automatic update is sent to your network then, click on "share this event"

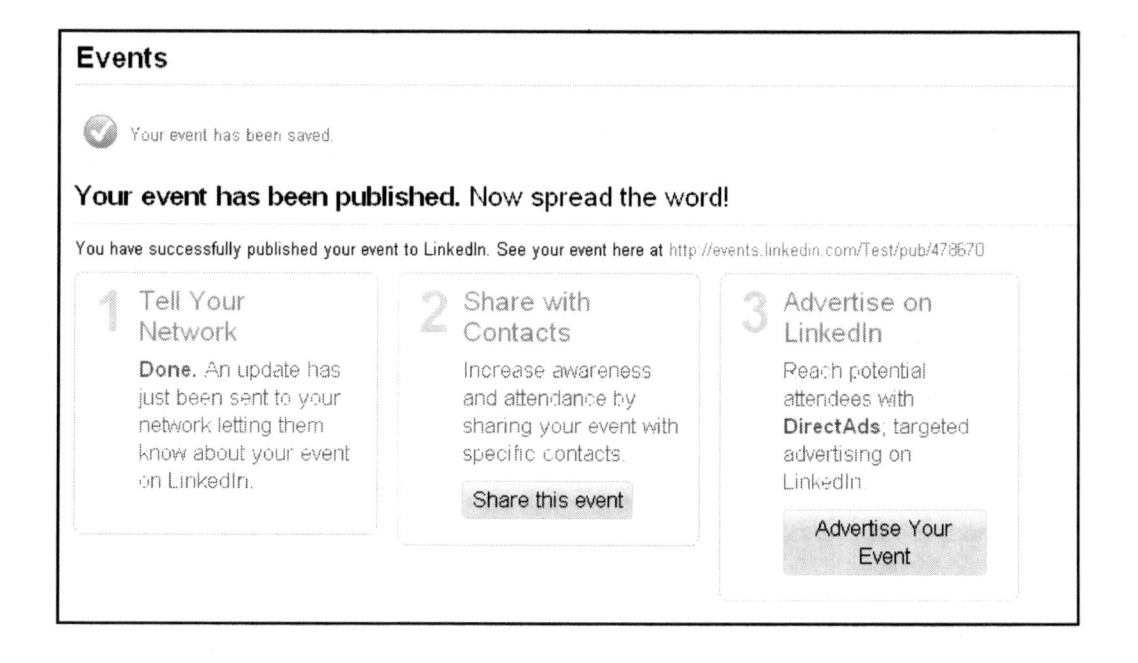

At this point you will be asked to write a message to your connections, inviting them to your event. You can use the standard "I found "x" event on Linkedin and thought you might be interested in going," but I recommend you write a personal note.

Send Message   Cancel

To:

From: Karen

Subject: LinkedIn Event: Test

found Test on LinkedIn Events and thought you might be interested in going!

Next click into the "To" box and you will be able to select connections to invite. You can share the event with up to 50 of your connections. Use the drop down menu to narrow the list by location or industry.

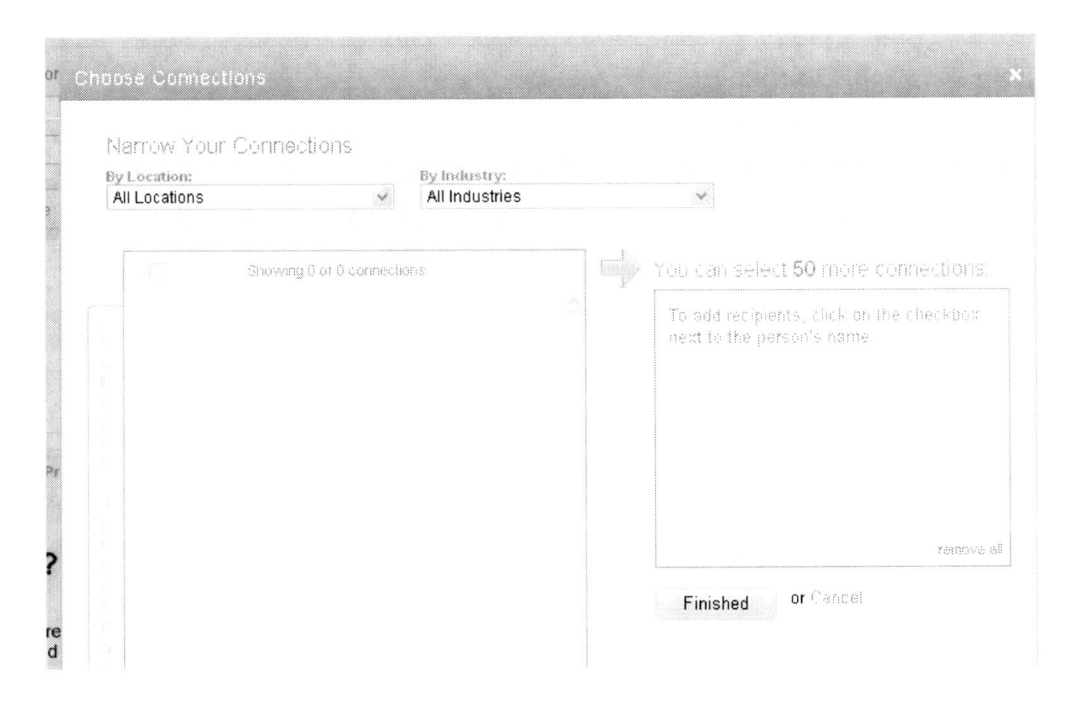

Chapter 12: Add video to your profile

LinkedIn is a great resource for promoting yourself, your products and services. A great enhancement to your LinkedIn profile is to add video. Why video? People LOVE videos, they give a sense of who and what you are. Imagine you are looking for a job and can post a video of yourself talking about your qualifications for certain positions or you are a salesperson who can show, through video, the benefits of your company's product or service right on your profile?

Adding video to your profile is easy. There are a couple of different applications that allow you to add video, Slideshare and Google Presentation. These are powerful tools and ones I've used myself for years.

Adding Video Using Google Presentation

In some respects I have I found it easier to use the Google presentation application than the Slideshare application however, Slideshare allows you to place 3 different videos on your profile in thumbnails, whereas the Google presentation app only allows you to show one presentation at a time. The Slideshare app also allows you to have the video play immediately upon landing on your profile—the Google Presentation does not. Both applications require you to upload your videos to YouTube prior to placing them into the application. In addition, the Google video will only be present if you are **logged in to your gmail account.** Not all of us are logged in all the time on gmail.

As I mentioned, you must have your video loaded to YouTube prior, and in order to use the Google Presentation application you will need to set up a Gmail account, but it's easy and free.

Here are the step by step instructions to add video with the Google Presentation app to your LinkedIn profile:

1. Login to LinkedIn

2. Go to the top right where it says "more"

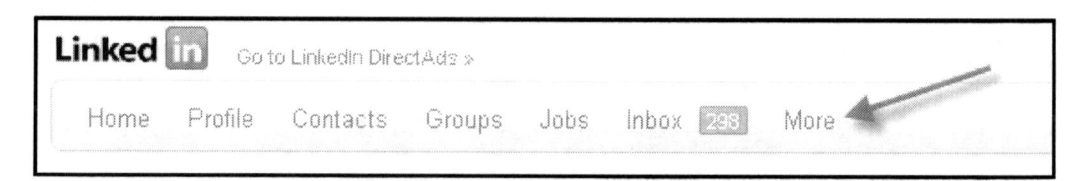

3. Go to the my applications or browse applications area

4. Add the Google Presentations application—make sure you check the boxes next to "Display on my profile", "Display on my home page", click "add application"

5. Click the "Create Presentation" button in the center of the screen (You must have a gmail address that you can use)

6. On the Google presentation screen go to the upper left and click on "untitled presentation" and change the name—to make it faster to find your video change the name to the title of your video.

7. On the main navigation bar select Insert > Video from the main menu

8. It will bring up a box that links to YouTube and from there you type in your video's title and your video should show up

9. Click on your video and say "add to presentation"—it will appear as a small thumbnail so drag out the sides to make it full screen

10. Go to the upper right corner and select publish/embed

11. Click "Save & Close" in the upper right corner

12. Go back to your LinkedIn Google presentation window, refresh the screen and your presentation should show up in the left window.

Select the presentation and click "Post to Profile"

You also have the option to "send to your network." You can promote the video to your Linkedin connections.

Chapter 13: The Power of Recommendations

As a professional, you know the power of personal testimonials or recommendations. People want to work/connect with people who have a track record of positive relationships with their clients and co-workers.

The LinkedIn Recommendation process starts in one of three ways:

- Unsolicited: When viewing the profile of any of your direct connections, a "Recommend This Person" link is clearly displayed at the top of the profile. You can click on that link to give an unsolicited Recommendation.

- Requested: You can request Recommendations from your direct connections (refer to example/screenshot below).

- Reciprocated: Whenever you accept a Recommendation from someone, LinkedIn will present you with the option of recommending that person as well. You should decide on a case by case basis whether or not you want to reciprocate or to simply send a thank you note for receiving the recommendation.

How do I ask for a recommendation?

Go to your profile page and click "Ask for a recommendation"

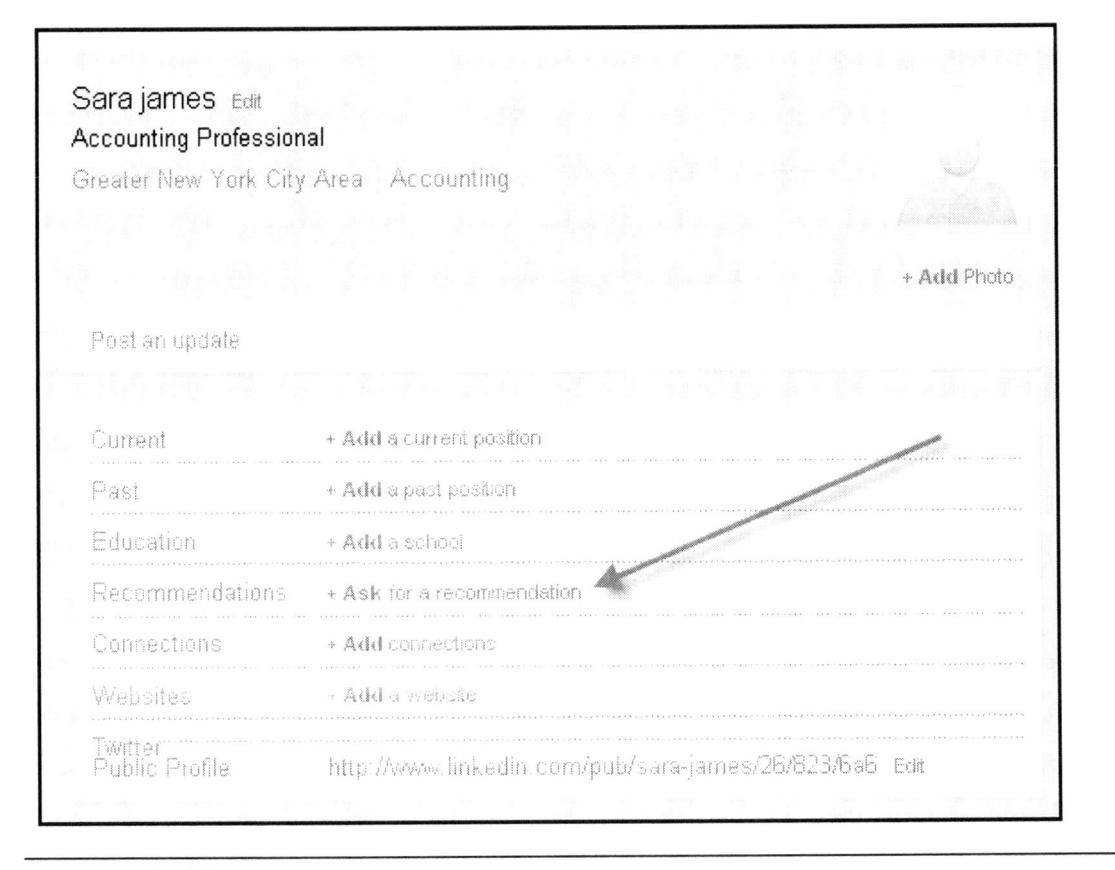

After you click "Get Recommended" this screen will come up:

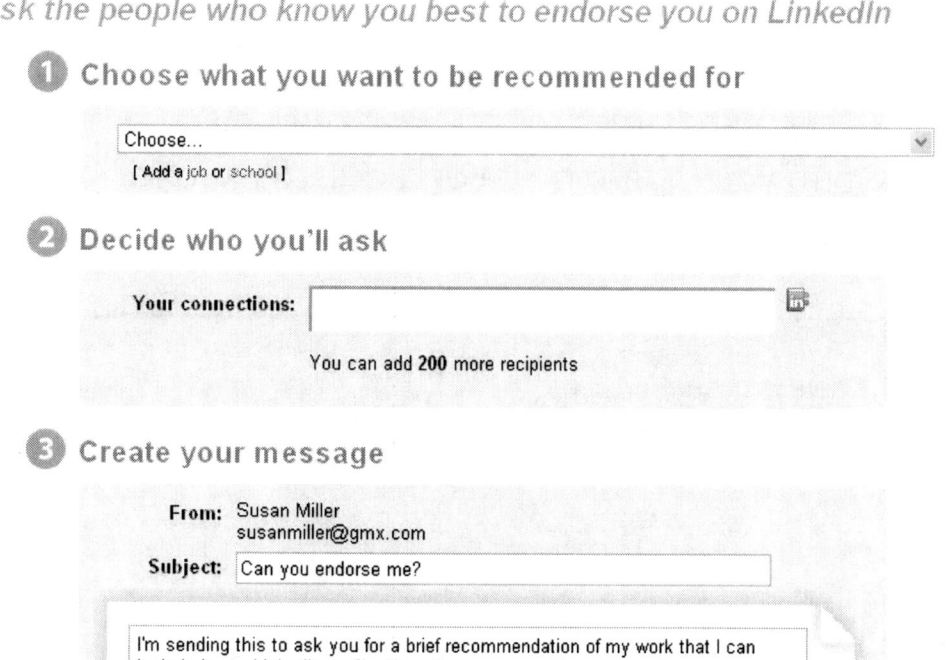

This is where you can choose what you want to be recommended for and by whom. After you've determined what and who, you will need to create a personal message.

Just like the connection invitations, there is a "stock" message that Linkedin provides. And, just like the connection invitations, I suggest you personalize this area and ask for a specific recommendation for a specific project or position. That way the person doesn't have to think about what to write. It makes it easier for them to recommend you.

Tips for requesting Recommendations:

- ➢ **Create a polite recommendation request.**
- ➢ **Give people some context as to why you're making the request (a project, a position, service provider...).**
- ➢ **Only ask a recommendation from individuals who know you or your work well enough to feel comfortable recommending you and have the basis for doing so.**
- ➢ **Remember, you're asking for a favor. The person you're contacting is in no way obligated.**
- ➢ **Make sure that the recommendations you display on your profile are good quality.**

I also suggest you don't just ask for recommendations but you give them as well. After you've formed connections, take the time to write each of them a recommendation and then ask for one in return. People are much more willing to write you a recommendation if you are willing to write one for them as well.

Tips for writing good quality Recommendations:

- **Be specific, talk about the person's strengths, skills and competencies.**
- **Talk about Results, Achievements (quantify)**
- **Tell how you know the person (colleague, business partner, service provider... it gives weight to your recommendation.**
- **Don't over-do it – If you think someone is exceptional, extraordinary or the very best in his/her field, than by all means say so, but don't go on and on about it.**
- **Be concise – LinkedIn has a 3,000 character limit on the length of Recommendations and you shouldn't reach it**

Recommendations are powerful. Ask for them judiciously and give them generously when deserved!

Chapter 14: Using Questions and Answers

The goal of LinkedIn Answers is to allow professionals to exchange expertise. Now imagine for a moment being able to ask a question to your network or the entire LinkedIn network for that matter and draw on the expertise and experience of tens of millions of people! This is exactly what LinkedIn Answers was designed for, and best of all, it's a free service available to the entire LinkedIn Community.

Word of caution: You should not use LinkedIn Answers as a way to create a personal advertisement for yourself, your product or service. Inappropriate questions include asking for a direct contact, posting a shameless plug for your product or service, or posting inappropriate content not suitable for public viewing. Again it bears repeating that with LinkedIn you are dealing with a professional crowd. So it isn't the place to ask for their favorite recipe. Ask that on Facebook!

In addition, *answering* questions is a good way to contribute some knowledge and to start being recognized in your field, industry or in your area of expertise.

To access the "answers" area, go to the top of the screen and click on "more".

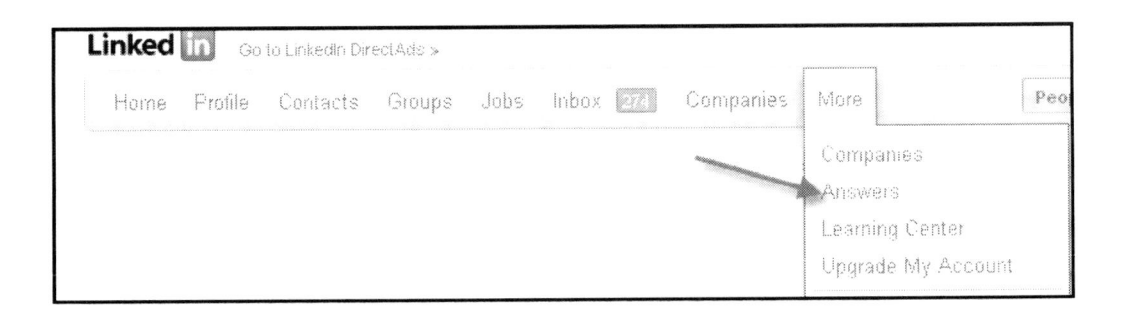

From here you can either ask a question or find questions to answer:

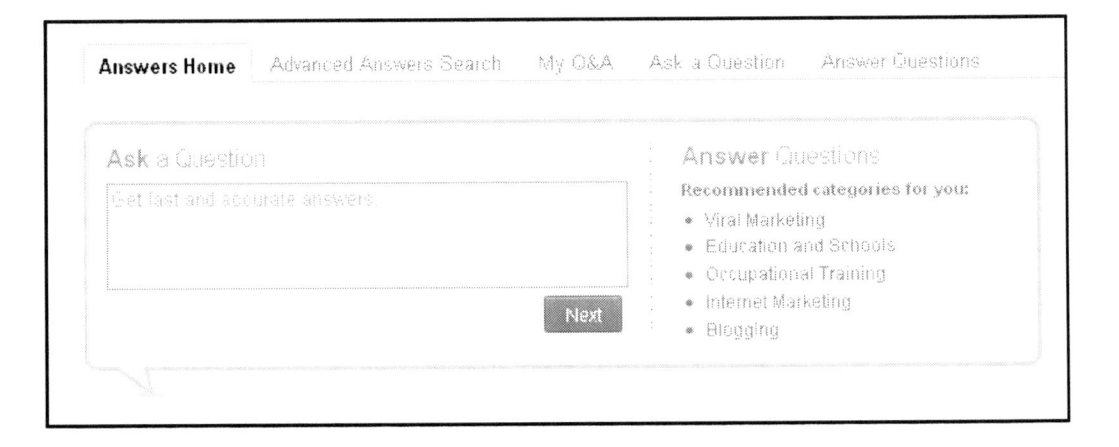

To find questions to answer click on Answer Questions tab and browse through all the current open questions, with the default sorting being questions from people that are in your LinkedIn network.

You can browse by Category listed on the right side of the Answers page, even go through the subcategories until you come across a question that's in line with your area of expertise.

If you intend to start asking questions of your own, it would be a good idea to spend some time looking through the list of questions and see how people are asking and answering questions.

Browse

Administration

Business Operations

Business Travel

Career and Education

Conferences and Event Planning

Finance and Accounting

Financial Markets

Government and Non-Profit

Health

Hiring and Human Resources

International

Law and Legal

Management

Marketing and Sales

Non-Profit

Personal Finance

Product Management

Professional Development

Startups and Small Businesses

Asking a Question

Whether it's a question pertaining to what you do, a project you're planning to start, or something that you need some insight and guidance on, LinkedIn is the place to start. Post your question and have the community help you.

Your LinkedIn question is available for up to seven days from the time you post the question on the site. You can always reopen your question later for more answers.

Fair Warning: LinkedIn prohibits using the Answers page for posting jobs, announcing your job search, or openly requesting people to connect with you. LinkedIn takes that warning very seriously and if you post such things, the questions will be deleted and your account (if you do it more than once) may be subject to suspension or closure.

Tips for getting the most and the best responses:

After you come up with your questions, take a moment to consider the best way to present your question in order to get useful responses.

- Use the right keywords in your question
- Use the appropriate category(ies) for your question
- Keep your question as simple as possible
- Engage your audience ex: How would you do X in this situation?
- Keep your question clean and readable – avoid spelling mistakes

Chapter 15: Using Linkedin Ads

Linkedin offers another way to get your message out to your target market: Linkedin Direct ads. These are paid advertisements that show up on member profiles:

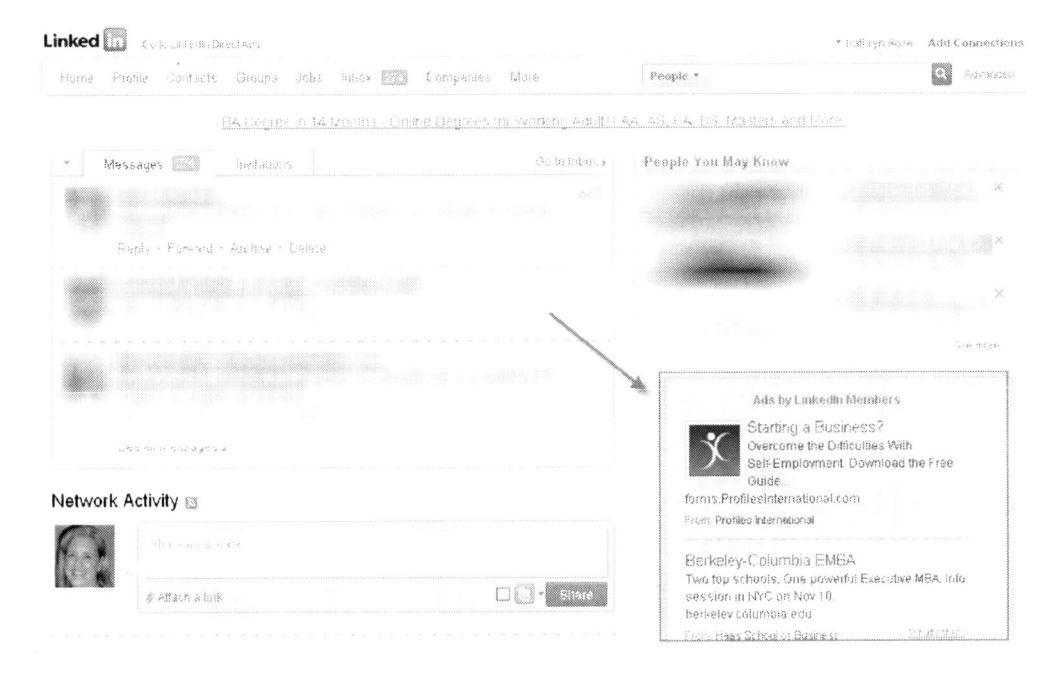

Your ads may show up in any of the ad placements on the site, including the medium rectangle ad on LinkedIn profile pages and the LinkedIn home page.

As with any other type of advertising campaign, I recommend before you get started placing ads on Linkedin you ask yourself a few questions:

1. What am I trying to accomplish? Are you trying to increase traffic to your website? Attendance at an event? Awareness of a product or service?

2. Who is my target audience? As you will see below Linkedin gives you the opportunity to target your advertising efforts.

3. What is my budget? I would not embark on any kind of an online campaign without knowing this number. While the minimum budget is $10.00 per day you will see once you begin to target your ads, the price per click or per impression moves higher. I recommend starting small and growing once you find an ad that is driving traffic.

Designing your campaign

Start by designing a headline and a call to action (this is an example of best practices from the Linkedin site):

The ads that perform best are relevant to the target audience and are written with clear, compelling words:

- ***Choose words that grab the attention*** *of your target audience and clearly explain what you offer. People use LinkedIn in ways that differ from other websites, so put yourself in your audience's shoes as you're creating your ads.*
- *Give people a **reason to take notice** and click to learn more by highlighting special offers, unique benefits, whitepapers, free trials or demos.*
- *Include **strong call-to-action phrases** like Try, Download, Sign up, or Request a Quote.*
- ***Include an image*** *with your ad that's relevant to what you offer. The maximum size of the image is 50 pixels wide by 50 pixels high, so be sure that the contents of your image are readable at this size.*
- *Be sure to review the advertising guidelines for details on what's acceptable to include in your ad.*

 **Effective**	 **Less Effective**

Need a Corporate Caterer?
Gourmet catering for private parties.
Affordable prices. Get a free quote.
www.TastyCorpCatering.com

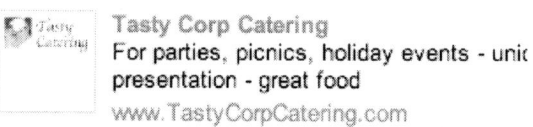

Tasty Corp Catering
For parties, picnics, holiday events - uni(
presentation - great food
www.TastyCorpCatering.com

What works well:

- *This headline clearly describes the products or services offered. Try an ad variation with a question in the headline to engage people.*
- *This description lists clear benefits and suggests a strong call-to-action.*

What could be improved:

- *The logo and the text within the image are too small and hard to read.*
- *This headline displays the company name rather than a word or phrase describing the service or key benefits of the service.*
- *This description does not use complete sentences and proper punctuation.*

When I am consulting clients on beginning an advertising campaign, I always recommend that several different ads with different headlines, calls to action etc. are created to test the responsiveness. I also recommend that it is wise to test different "landing" pages for the ads to see what content drives conversions (sales, sign ups for events, etc) more effectively. You may want to consider hiring an online advertising expert to create these for you.

One of the great things about Linkedin ads is that you can use targeting tools to hone in on your ideal audience:

Linked in DirectAds (beta)   Welcome, Kathryn

Target Your Audience

Your audience can be narrowed by using the targeting options below:

○ Show ad to all LinkedIn members

◉ Target audience by category (select up to 4):

Your Target Audience:
83,076,466
LinkedIn Members

☐ Company Size

☐ Job Function

☐ Industry

☐ Seniority

☐ Gender

☐ Age

☐ Geography

Total Target Audience: 83,076,466 Members

☑ **Also reach LinkedIn members on other websites through the** LinkedIn Audience Network

Checking the box next to each category expands the window so you can see all of the options. Here are examples of target areas available to improve the effectiveness of your campaign:

- By geography – Limit the geography of your campaign if your products or services only appeal to users in certain countries or cities.
- By job function and seniority – Target by job function if you want to limit your ads to people who are in one of 18 broad job functions like Medical Practice, Publishing or Real Estate.
- By industry and company size – When targeting people who work in a certain industry, be careful not to inadvertently leave out industries that fit your target audience. For example, if your main target is "Publishing", you may also want to include "E-Learning", "Internet", "Newspapers", "Online Media" and "Writing and Editing".
- By gender and age

Remember though, the more targeted, the less of an audience and the more expensive your ads will be.

Once you have created your campaign it is time to set a budget. Here you have two options:

CPC – Pay per "click" where you pay each time your ad is clicked

CPM – cost per thousand, you pay for each 1000 impressions.

Many people ask me which is better. In my opinion unless you have a time sensitive offer, I always use CPM, it is less expensive and you get more eyeballs on your ad. CPM is also great for a branding or awareness campaign.

How do I set my daily budget?

Linkedin says: *If you're just getting started with DirectAds, we suggest that you enter a bid that's within the Suggested Bid Range. The Suggested Bid Range is an estimate of the current competing bids by other advertisers. The higher your bid within the range, the more likely it is for your ad to be shown and receive clicks.*

How it works: You set a bid for each of your campaigns. A real-time auction is run each time a LinkedIn user visits a

page that contains an ad unit. If the user falls into your targeting options, your ad will be entered into this auction along with the bids of other advertisers. If you do not enter a bid within the suggested range, your ad will be less likely to beat other advertisers' bids in the auction, resulting in fewer or no impressions or clicks. Remember that the bid you choose is the maximum you're willing to pay, and we will discount your click or impression so that you're only paying the minimum necessary to beat the advertiser below you.

Your daily budget is the maximum amount that you are willing to spend each day. We display your ads at different rates during the day depending on when LinkedIn users are active on the website -- for example, 50% of your budget might be spent in the morning, 30% in the afternoon, and 20% overnight. Once your Daily Budget is reached, your ads will stop showing for that day. Also, note that since most people visit LinkedIn on weekdays, you're more likely to spend your Daily Budget *during the week than over the weekend.*

Tracking your ad performance:

Linkedin provides reporting and analysis for all of your ad campaigns. To assess how your ads are performing, it is recommended to use the CTR (click through rate) percentage. This is how many times users have "clicked through" to your link. In general, a performing ad will have a CTR of over .02%

If your CTR is lower than this, you should create another ad with a different headline, call to action etc. Linkedin allows you to test up to 10 different ads within a single campaign. You may also want to adjust your target audience so that your ad becomes more relevant and in return may receive more clicks.

Chapter 16: Listing your company on Linkedin

In the past few years, Linkedin has vastly improved the way companies are represented on the network. You can add a company, and offer a snapshot of the organization in terms of number of employees, industry, etc. You can also "follow" a company and be provided with updates when company news is updated.

To set up a company go to the menu bar click "companies" and then "add a company."

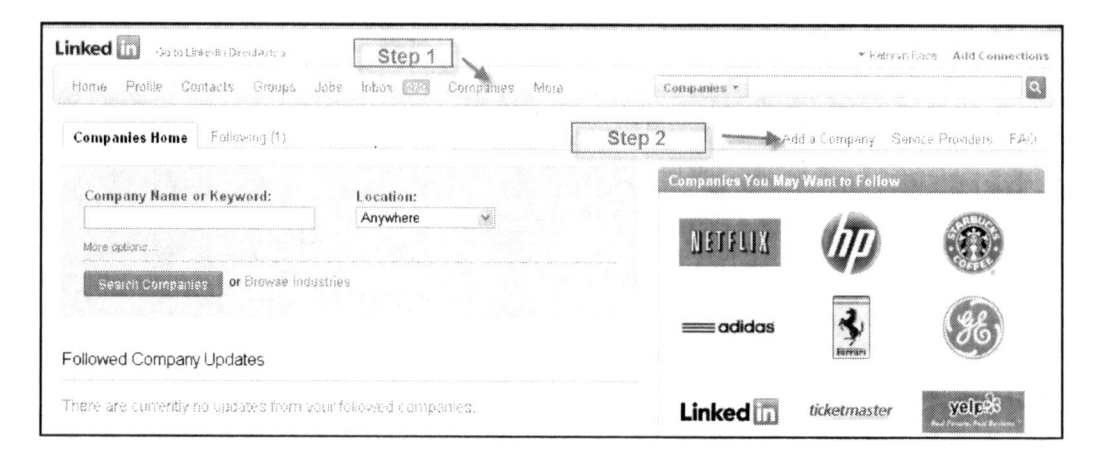

You will then be asked to add in your company name

---

and your email address at the company:

You will also be asked to assert that you are in fact authorized to set up this company account. It is important that you do not set up a company if you are not the owner or an authorized representative.

An email is sent to your account asking you to confirm your company set up request:

Completing your company profile:

You will be asked to fill in all of the information about your company, the type, number of employees, URL, etc.

You can even enter your company's blog RSS feed, Twitter id and decide whether or not you want news about your company shared on the platform:

Once you have completed this, click "publish" and your company profile will be available on the network.

Chapter 17: Following Companies, Users or Discussions

In the recent past, Linkedin added a great feature that allows you to in essence track people, conversations and companies through the platform. They call it "following." You may have heard about following people in reference to the social media platform Twitter. This works in a similar fashion except you can't just follow random people, you have to be connected to them in some way.

It works differently with companies. You can follow any company you wish and I cover that later in this chapter.

By default, Linkedin has you "following" all of your 1st degree connections.

How do I find out who I'm following and who is following me?

Click on Groups on the top navigation bar in LinkedIn.

From the tabs that appear on the top of the page, select Following.

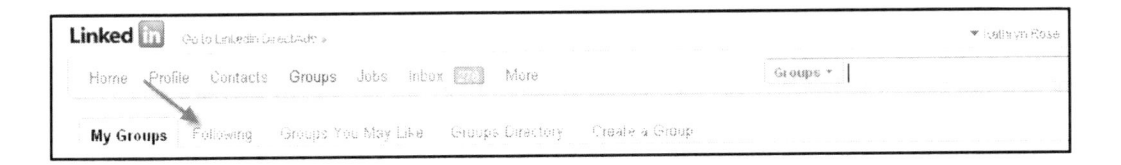

You'll see in the top-left corner of the page a list of links, including "People I'm Following" , "My Followers," and "Discussions I'm Following."

Click on either of those links to see who you're following, and who's following you. You'll notice that under each person, you have the option to follow/unfollow, and to get email alerts:

If you choose to get email alerts, you'll get an email every time they do anything on LinkedIn. This is a good feature if you really want to keep a close eye on someone, but not if you just want to be connected.

Following discussions:

You can also follow "discussions" in the group area. Let's say someone asked a question about a topic that you would like to know as well. When you find a discussion that interests you, click to enter the discussion and you will see this bar come up:

Click on the Follow tab and you are now going to receive updates every time someone posts a new answer within that discussion.

Following Companies on Linkedin

When you follow a company, you can keep up to date

on what is happening within any organization. You can find valuable information such as, career postings, news releases, to whom you are already connected in that organization and which degree of connection they are. You can even see statistics on the employees of the company such as, job function composition, years of experience, degrees and which universities employees attended.

The option to follow companies can be very valuable. Below are some of the ways you can use the Follow company feature for yourself and your business:

1. **Sales and Business Development:**

    A virtual treasure trove of information can be gathered for sales people by following prospective or current client companies. Using the follow company feature you can find out who the decision makers are, see who has moved in to the decision maker role or just as importantly, who moved out.

You can find out what is being said about the organization in the news media. Are there new products being launched? Are they opening a new office in your territory?

You always have a leg up if you do research on a prospect and you keep your accounts by staying current on your client's needs. Following companies can provide you with current information to make it easier for you to keep tabs on your client base.

2. Find Employment:

It doesn't take a genius to see the value in the Follow company feature for those who want to find work at a particular organization. Just like the sales and business development folks, you can find out who the people are that may be in a position to hire you.

You also get automatically notified when there are new job openings. To get the notifications, you set your Follow Company alerts to receive an email with the company updates.

Once you find the position you would like to apply for, check the employee statistics area (which is part of the FREE version) and you can even find out what kind of qualifications you may need to have to compete with other job seekers.

3. Recruiters:

Recruiters can use the information they get from the follow company feature, to find out who is leaving a company, what positions are available and who the people are that are making the hiring decisions. As a recruiter, you can follow companies on your target list or by following your competitors you can glean information that could point you toward the hiring trends and practices in an organization. You can also find talent to place into open positions.

There are many other ways you can use the Follow company feature and I am sure that as time passes, Linkedin will come up with more ways to help you find information and gain a competitive edge.

Chapter 18: Creating Your Linkedin Strategy

In the very beginning of the book, I asked you to think about what your strategy was for using Linkedin. It bears repeating at the end of the book. Take the time to decide what you want to get out of LinkedIn. Is it projects, a job change, clients, service providers? All of these and more are possible when you dedicate focused and consistent time and attention to your connections.

It is often easy to get caught up in simply growing your network. But the power is when you actually engage with your network. I try to set aside 15 minutes daily to actively discover what is happening in the lives of the people in my network. Visit your LinkedIn home pages, groups and the answers area regularly. Subscribe to your LinkedIn network updates via RSS feed or follow users discussion and companies and stay current. When your connections post an update, you may want to use this as an opportunity to reach out PERSONALLY (yes, I said personally) via e-mail or telephone for a quick catch-up.

And last, once a month, set aside a couple hours and explore the contacts you already have, find out who they are, what they have to offer and what they are up to, and remember that each of their networks is ripe for valuable contacts.

As you can only imagine, there is so much more to using the power of LinkedIn to build, grow and manage your professional network. I hope you found this information helpful and I would be pleased if you would connect with me on Linkedin:

http://linkedin.com/in/katkrose

To your Linkedin success!

Chapter 19: Checklist for Success

Here is an easy to follow checklist that will help you get on the right path and help you get the most out of LinkedIn.

- ☐ Optimize your profile with Keyword rich:
  - ○ Titles
  - ○ Job Descriptions
  - ○ Company summary
- ☐ Be sure to include your website links – using the "other" category and include keyword rich description of the link
  - ○ Link to your blog, Facebook and any other pages that are relevant to you or your profession
- ☐ Add your Twitter ID
- ☐ Assign a custom URL to make it easier to add to your website, email signature, etc.
- ☐ Search and ask for connections from people you know FIRST
- ☐ Add the following applications:
  - ○ Slideshare
  - ○ Company Buzz/Twitter
  - ○ Events
  - ○ Blog Link or WordPress
  - ○ Reading List for Amazon

☐ Go to LinkedIn at least once per week and add something under the "What are you working on" area to keep your connections updated on you or your company's activities.

☐ Search for relevant, active groups and join them. Make sure you engage by:
- ○ Asking relevant questions
- ○ Provide good and relevant content
- ○ Asking for connections with other members

☐ At least once per week write a recommendation for another person and ask for a recommendation from others.

☐ Go into the "Answers" area regularly and search for questions where you can provide expertise.

Other books by Kathryn Rose

Step by Step Guides to :

Facebook for Business

Twitter for Business

SEO/Video Marketing for Business

The Parent's Guide to Facebook

Offers parents a more in depth step by step guide to privacy and, including monitoring your children's online activities and how to protect them on Facebook.

The Tweens/Teens Guide to Facebook

Offers children the tools to help guide them through setting up and interacting on the world's largest social network with privacy and safety in mind.

The Grandparent's Guide to Facebook

Great for grandparents who want to keep in touch with their grandkids. Includes mcdule on "Skype" a free service that allows free video and audio calls to stay connected.

CPSIA information can be obtained at www.ICGtesting.com
Printed in the USA
LVOW09s1631290615

444296LV00007B/353/P